THE PAUSE EFFECT

THE PAUSE EFFECT

NOW YOU CAN
LEAD AND BELONG

MEGAN BROKER

MANUSCRIPTS
PRESS

THE PAUSE EFFECT
Now You Can Lead and Belong

ISBN   979-8-88926-041-7 *Paperback*

979-8-88926-040-0 *eBook*

979-8-88926-042-4 *Hardcover*

Okino Pokino!

Contents

Introduction

It was a bluebird day in Washington, DC, as we call them in the mountains of Colorado. One where the sky is vast and open to warmth, the sun offers kindness and hope, and the temperature provides an indication of the season to come. Early spring felt more like late spring, with the blooms creating a bit of seasonal buzz. And for the first time, I was finally meeting my colleague in person, which felt long overdue and more like a reunion with an old friend.

Due to the pandemic way of meeting, connecting, working, and engaging, we had only met over video, yet we had established so many connections. The aroma of coffee on a slow drip was a stark contrast to the pace of our conversation. We sped into a deep discussion, moving quickly past pleasantries and platitudes due to our many previously revealed commonalties—we are both executive coaches, we share an alma mater, we are former consultants, and we are both parents, to name a few. He shared he was writing a book about a health-related topic with which he has intimate first-hand experience.

As we talked about his book project and went deeper, I shared that if I ever wrote a book, I would title it *Leadership Lessons Learned from Blending a Family—or an Attempt at Such* and quickly laughed. My friend wasn't laughing. He leaned forward, and I knew this was his way of telling me that my laugh wasn't letting me off the hook. He was waiting for further context.

I explained how blended families are like a highly matrixed organization. The org charts are confusing, individuals report to multiple managers, and the roles lack clarity of success measures. Communication and clarity are critical and often not as timely and specific as needed. Add to that, working in two different companies full time at the same time, holding two very different positions with diverse stakeholders and skillsets, is impossible. Yet being a parent and engaging in a relationship with someone other than the other parent to that child or those children, demands you do exactly that: hold varied jobs in vastly different companies with varying success measures and inconsistent performance partners evaluating your engagement and performance.

As a divorced mom of one child, I hold a position in that company. As the wife of a previously divorced man with three kids, I also hold a position in that company. The positions are wildly different. In the first, I may as well be the CEO; in the second, I'm more like a corporate auditor. In the former, I have autonomy and set the tone; in the latter, I need a variety of technical proficiencies to be competent, and the essential skills and capabilities are highly refined.

My friend stopped me and said, "Do it! Seriously, Megan, do it!"

As we talked, I became acutely aware the clients I had been working with on their leadership challenges faced many of the same opportunities for self-awareness and growth as I had when I went through my divorce and then created a blended family when my ex-husband and I each added a partner. This opportunity surfaced again when I started dating my now-husband and joining that blended family with his ex-wife, her partner, and his kids.

My entry to blended families was much like joining a new company—one in the midst of a major transformation at that. When I started dating my now-husband, Jeff, it was like entering a company experiencing turbulent times. I married that wonderful man while the company was still navigating stormy seas. When I previously navigated my divorce, I was clear in my purpose and intentions. However, I lacked that clarity entering the new blended family. If my then-boyfriend and his former wife were the senior leaders of this new company I was joining, I did not hear a clear vision nor a strategy going in, and my perspective with whatever was happening lacked alignment. We all had the underlying assumption that everything would be done in the best interest of the kids, but what that approach looked like differed greatly among all of us.

The themes that surface in blended families, in the roles and blurred lines of those roles—empathy, conflicts, and working to a goal of cohesion—are a lens through which we can see how we can navigate our leadership positions.

Ironically, blended families have a slightly higher success rate of 30 percent versus success of mergers and acquisitions of companies that stall at an average 20 percent rate (US Census Bureau 2023; Siddiqui, Abdul, and Farooq 2019). Sufficient to say, both are difficult environments to navigate and succeed in integration. But both share the need to be clear in ones' values and brand and the need to recognize moments to show up authentically.

As I thought about the stories from leaders and people being led I've worked with, I realized they all mimicked the experiences I had in blending families. Moments arise that demonstrate who we are to others or are aligned to who we intend to be, but we might miss the opportunity to pause and ensue alignment.

My success on one side of blending families is markedly higher than on the other side, which is a cause for awareness of distinctions and differences in how I have shown up—intentionally and unintentionally. In the chapters that follow, you'll learn I am still seeking my own belonging in my role of stepmom to Robyn, Corey, and Scott seventeen years into the marriage. I've learned in my quest for this belonging while learning that strong parenting—"Do it because I said so"—had to make way for deeper understanding and conversations about the whys. This shift in blended family parenting, trying to gain collaboration and connection and move away from "stepmonsters," can be applied to shifts in individuals as they take on new roles in their work.

Like many parents and stepparents, leaders have to navigate their new positions of power or positions and work to create a seamless transition from one structure to the next. Some see themselves holding very senior titles but fail to see themselves as "leaders." Conversely, some see the titles they hold and assume others see them as leaders. But they aren't.

Parents, stepparents, managers, individual contributors, C-suite executives, and all in the mix of this continuum have the opportunity to lead. The behaviors, consistency, and alignment of our language signals who we are and why people will or will not follow us. Taking inventory of this to ensure consistency in how we show up is critical to narrowing the gap between intent—what we hope others will think of us—and impact—the reality of how others see us. More succinctly said: If your title and position were taken away, who would follow you, and why?

We have long believed that as leaders rise in organizations, it gets lonelier. They put in place a filter, a distance, a separation to be effective in their role the more senior they become. In fact, they are expected to put those in place. Yet we know the higher a leader goes in the organization, the more disconnected they become from what is really happening *in* the organization, creating a gap in how deeply they can impact the organization. What really needs to happen is *not* to implement the filter, not create a separation, not show up as who they *think* the title demands, but instead to show up authentically connected to who they as people command; to belong.

The phrase "It's lonely at the top" is true because leaders who don't know what to say, how to say it, or whom to share a connection with often find themselves isolated and lonely at the top of the organization. As I navigated my divorce with a polarizing, at the time, "why" for the divorce in a highly connected town, I felt this same uncertainty. When I began dating my now-husband a few years later, I experienced the same feelings of uncertainty and isolation of who to talk to, who to engage with, what I could say, and what I shouldn't say.

My divorce offered the gift of it being mine. It was my proverbial organization that was going through turbulent times, and I could control the narrative, so much so that I could choose how I wanted others to experience me. In my choice not to share the "why" of my divorce, people made assumptions. I took a lot of character hits as others guessed theories and casted blame erroneously. I was okay with that, because I knew the truth and only had to show up consistent to my core value of integrity. The high road was lonely, but I was definitely on it.

After a successful twenty-five-year run in corporate roles across many industries and positions, I started my own executive coaching practice to engage with work that is meaningful and with clients who are ready to do the work. I began hearing more often the challenge leaders are having to define what the future of work looked like in a post pandemic, lockdown world. This challenge is also creating awareness to their own connection and belonging. The hybrid in-person and remote conundrum hits a nerve of balance, preference, autonomy, connection, importance of espoused corporate culture and values, all after we opened our homes and our families on video without reservation. We got to know each other's pets, living spaces, families, or the silence of living alone, and now we are caught in how to continue that connection and not abruptly shift the focus to the need for deliverables, execution, efficiencies, and continuing to do the work that allows us to have jobs.

We have an enlightened generation driving for more: more awareness, more equity, more balance, more opportunity, more inclusion. We have organizations with affinity groups meeting the collective needs of identities, employee bases finding connections, and those in senior roles being called on to act, to demonstrate commitment, and to be real. Research tells us that employee retention is posing significant challenges and signaling that people are restless and taking charge of their own professional happiness (Tessema et al. 2022). From the employee perspective, the challenge is how do I identify and find the leaders who create the culture for me to thrive, who deliver on what they say, who align work and expectations to their espoused company values, and who I consistently experience who they are as leaders? This reconciliation has never existed before now. And it is a loud call to action that what we have always done is not enough to step into the next position.

As I join in this dance with those in senior roles who are looking at their impact as a leader, not just as a person in a position, we spend time engaging around those deliberate decisions that feed their soul—when they do what feels right versus what they think they should do. And we get into the messy work of what has been modeled for them in those ivory tower positions and how that impacted them. The vision of reaching a level, promoting to a position as indicators of importance has shifted to the impact one is making as a measure of success. The days of getting "there" at all costs have given way to getting "there" with all the people on the bus, buckled in, going to the same destination and abiding by the rules of the road.

The Pause Effect is the impact you can have in finding your own belonging, owning the clarity of your values and what you want to be known for, so when those moments surface for you to act true to your intent, your clarity comes through. Even when the stakes and emotions are high, they do not overtake the moment when you pause, recognize the opportunity, and act aligned to who *you* are. It's awareness of your own reactions, emotions, tendencies, and similarities or differences with others. Be intentional of what to do with that awareness. Often, there is a cultural disconnect in driving organizations to push for results and deliverables. *The Pause Effect* is a difference maker. Pausing allows us to reflect on the clarity of our values and the choices in front of us—to be aware. The effect is that we remain true to those values; to be intentional and prevent high stakes and strong emotions from overtaking to respond instinctively and immediately. The chapters that follow will share how and why *The Pause Effect* payoffs are big. We can do this.

How are you taking inventory of the verbalization of what you stand for and aligning your actions to those statements? The office, physical or virtual, is not the only playing field for this. Like the framed poster on the walls of lobbies and offices intended to make us pause and think or to inspire us to be aware states with a lone canoe in a serene lake at dawn: "Integrity is what you do when no one is watching." So, when you are in different situations, how are you intentionally listening to who you say you are and outwardly connecting your words and actions to authentically being you? We rarely take the time to pause and take note; even less so to discuss with someone else and get some honest thought-provoking discussions about why we keep doing what has been modeled, despite the insufficiency of that approach. But if we don't start, we will fail to move the needle on who we strive to be, whether that is as a positional executive role, a leader, a board member, a parent, or a coach. The role is agnostic. Your impact and power are yours to harness and unleash.

What systems are you a part of that you can pause and reflect on how you are showing up and how that aligns to your values? If you are a senior or executive leader in a company, this book is for you. This is a nudge to slow your roll and look in to grab the power a short pause offers. If you are divorced, a member of a blended family, someone who has or anticipates navigating turbulent times, early in your career, late in your career, individual contributors, and seasoned executives, this book is for you. The power you hold is in being intentional in the moments that require awareness and discipline to pause—and identifying the frequency of those moments so you don't miss them. *The Pause Effect* will guide you to unlock and harness that power.

Each chapter will dive into challenges that I have faced in my dual family roles and are consistent with leaders in organizations. The chapters end with practice prompts to create awareness of the opportunities to be intentional and seize them. I have included intentionally blank pages after the practice prompts to reinforce the pause. They serve as a visible reminder to not let the moment slip without realizing you have a valuable moment to make a choice.

You made the choice to pick up this book. Now it's time to see where else you can make an intentional choice to create time, empower others, connect, engage, reflect, and diffuse. And all it takes is the decision to turn the page.

Pause to Show Up

"Between stimulus and response, there is a space. In that space lies our freedom and our power to choose our response. In our response lies our growth and our happiness."

—VIKTOR FRANKL

JEWISH-AUSTRIAN PSYCHIATRIST AND HOLOCAUST SURVIVOR

FOUNDER OF LOGOTHERAPY

The gray clouds offered a chill in the air with a low-hanging ceiling of dread. I was in year seven of what my five-year-old daughter told her class was my "selling drugs" career, but she told them not to worry, it was the "good kind of drugs." This represented my job as a pharmaceutical sales rep, and the "good drugs" were primarily allergy and asthma medications. My new district manager was spending the day riding with me to the doctors' offices I called on with the goal of supposedly getting to know me and how I worked my territory. The morning calls were fairly uneventful and about what I had expected covering studies, patient disease state, product efficacy, and insurance coverage—the typical routine of detailing your products to prescribing providers.

Midday, the district manager and I stopped for lunch. The restaurant was in a hotel and was under renovation while still open. The construction was a bit of a deterrent to the aesthetic appeal, leaving the lunch time crowd quite thin. As our voices echoed and our energy lagged, we discussed the challenges of the territory that went beyond shifting prescribing habits of doctors. The conversations moved to the manager asking me how many of these doctors I had a relationship with—those who I saw outside of work as friends, as golf partners to my husband, as parents of my kids' friends; those I would see socially. I thought about it and said probably ten. He went on to tell me he wanted me to go tell those ten that I was up for a trip to Hawaii and ask them to help me get there by writing more prescriptions for the drugs I represented.

Not being one who is known for a strong poker face, I have no doubts my eyes expressed my shock at this suggestion. I replied that I would not lie, nor would I ask for favors; that my job and the direction from our regional director was to promote our products based on research and benefits. He continued with his narrative about what I felt was a scam he wanted me to market. It escalated quickly when I asked for this direction in writing, since it was counter to what had been rolled out in the region. The manager stood up to tower over my seated position, pointed a finger in my face, and said loudly, "You will do it because I told you to do it," as he pivoted and left the restaurant.

Spoiler alert, I didn't do it, but we will talk more about that in "Pause for Your Journey."

The district manager had the ability to be a leader of me by virtue of his title and role relative to mine. Positions with titles like "district manager" and "regional director" have an implied "leader" in them. Ironically, many use the word "leader" without intention to describe the person in an organization who one reports up to; one who is the most senior (or a senior) person with management responsibility of a function or a department. But leadership is a capability, not a position. In my case, my manager lacked the capability. Good leaders set a clear vision and create the environment for others to deliver to the vision. They provide opportunities to build skill, increase capabilities, and hope that the vision is attainable. To truly guide, a leader requires followers. Leadership is a capability that anyone at any level can, and should, develop with intention. Followership is built on the journey, not at a pinnacle moment of promotion. I did not want to follow his lead.

Every person has their own leadership journey. There are demonstrated behaviors that differentiate those people in leadership level positions who have followers and those who do not. Satya Nadella interviewed for a computer science position at Microsoft in the early 1990s. After a grueling technical interview process and generating many answers, he thought he was finished. Instead, he was asked one more question: What would he do if he saw a child fall at a crossroad? His reply that he would run to the closest phone booth and call 911 earned him a "we are not hiring you" notice. The interviewer explained to him that if a child falls, they need to be picked up and hugged, and his response exposed his lack of empathy to do such. The interviewer went on to tell Nadella he needed to develop empathy—and this lesson stuck with him. As the current CEO of Microsoft, he has likely developed the behavior that represents empathy to navigate the rise to CEO. More importantly, he likely thinks about how he shows up in the moment and answers questions representing his true response (Jones 2019).

Robert Greenleaf coined "the servant as leader" in his essay of the same title exploring these leaders who show up to *serve* first versus those who *lead* first. The concept of being a servant—or serving others—is the highest priority. This theory moved hierarchical power to shared power in leading others by meeting them where they are, sharing the power, and increasing engagement in organizations. Serve the people and they will follow instead of tell the people to follow you and expect they will (Greenleaf 1970).

While this is important and undoubtedly a successful approach, it still misses out on the opportunity for "ob-servant leadership" because it shifts the focus to another person versus:

- Being so present with oneself that they are able to see the big and long-term impact before actioning;
- Being so present they are able to engage as their authentic self;
- Meeting others where they are and what they need while also getting what you as the leader need; and
- Feeding your soul too.

Our history and experiences shape how we have learned to lead. We pattern what has been modeled for us—what we see leaders do—and we mimic without further exploration to adapt until called to do so. This modeling shifts over time, and so does our experience of what we then model for others. Professors and researchers of leadership Andert, Alexakis, and Preziosi looked at a multi-generational leadership model and found that leaders establish an approach based on the events and impacts of what is happening as they are raised. As an example, generations who were entering the workforce at a time of war veterans returning and reentering upon their return brought the command-and-control hierarchical nature of the military with them. This style of leadership established a delineation between leaders and followers and how leadership demanded the higher-ups by position alone and not behavior and character. As the generations shift, world events change, and technology advances so do the leadership and employee norms. The events and shifts in culture create a pattern of leadership that serves the needs they have at the time but fails to adapt to who they are leading when that population evolves to a different generation. What individuals value and how they see themselves also evolves and calls to be defined (Andert, Alexakis, and Preziosi 2019).

Values are the core of our individual belief systems. They are our principles; our standards. They are what we use to measure others, tasks, opportunities, success, failure—pretty much everything. Values are also what motivate each of us. Many of our values are anchored in a story—an event, an upbringing, something tangible we can tell a story about how it came to be. Someone raised on a farm and having to work before going to school, then hurried home after the academic day to pitch in with more chores might value hard work. Someone who was raised without financial resources and faced hardship because of the scarcity might value financial security. Knowing your core values requires self-reflection, but this awareness is key to knowing how you want others to experience you. Your values shape how you interact with the outside world and others.

I often ask my clients what they want to be known for. What are the three things that no matter who I ask they would like the response to be consistent. This is your leadership brand: the behaviors that establish how others experience you. These behaviors are an outward expression of your core values. Your values drive your behaviors, and your behaviors drive how others experience you. When you are not intentional and clear about what your values are, your behaviors can be experienced as confusing or leave others without an understanding of why you do what you do. This lack of intentionality fails to establish a consistent brand and misses the opportunity (and call) to be clear about who you are as a leader and as a person.

I recently had a client tell me they held respect as a core value. This client leads a sales desk of a large private equity firm. He tells his team all the time that he will not tolerate anyone being rude—dishing it out or on the receiving end—no matter how big of a client they are. One client was extremely rude to one of his sales desk team members. He talked to the client and told them that yelling at the desk members is not an option and he would not allow it. Through his talking to the client, the team got a clear understanding of how their leader's values are actioned and that what he claims is important. For this leader, he had a decision to make in the moment when he found out what he states as important and tolerable was being challenged. He had an option to excuse the behavior, which would have diluted his espoused value of respect for the sake of the monetary value of the client. Instead, his action modeled a behavior to develop and coach the team on how to navigate the situation without backing out of taking a stand as the most senior person in the department. This development and modeling was a secondary benefit to his intentional choice.

Opportunities show up every day to pause and consider how you want to be experienced; intentionally act in alignment to your values and brand. Many "good" leaders skate past recognizing what others need them to be in the name of "servant leadership." Too many of these opportunities are rushed past, missing the "ob-servant" moment. What is at risk to hit the pause button? Moments are fleeting, and it is easy to trick yourself into thinking they are little and don't matter, but we all know the little things add up. The time will not lapse when you hit pause. So, in the moments you pause and take inventory, what are those data points telling us about your leadership and character?

Early career managers often tell me about the underperformers on their team. They tell story after story of how the individual has sent a report with the same mistakes each time. The manager notes the corrections and sends it back. The individual makes the actual corrections and sends it back to the manager for submission. This pattern repeats itself with each cycle of the task. And the individual is now being labeled an "under performer" because the manager is not clarifying what the individual should be learning, applying what they see from the corrections and fixing them before the next cycle of submission.

I was this early career manager once upon a time.

I was promoted into a position to lead a lot of volunteers to raise funds in an organization where I was once one of those volunteers. The previous manager and her assistant were a dynamic duo and had flawlessly run this program. They worked as a team and in unison. I wanted to follow their model, and I had a person to manage who was supposed to help me with this big job. But I was new to my role, and she was new to the organization, and that is where my model of what it was supposed to look like broke down. She was older than me and also junior to me. I had expectations that she would somehow figure out what I needed and how to keep all of the moving parts running on time and in synch. But the moving parts were not in sync and were creating a mess. So, like my clients in these roles, I actioned her exit. I fired her. The single biggest shame of my career was this act. I gave no indication it was going in this direction, and she had no way of knowing it was coming.

Like my clients, I did not communicate clearly what the role and expectations were. I gave input "hoping" she would get it (and hope is not a strategy!). Firing her took approval from my superiors, so it is curious that I did not receive coaching and upskilling from them. There was not a development of me; no dialogue or training about how to manage others and set clear expectations or deliver feedback. If I'd had a behavior to model, then I likely would have handled my situation differently. But when it comes down to it, my action was my decision, and I disconnected it from who I was, and I lacked clarity in what I wanted to build my brand to be.

I could have done any number of things, and I have come up with many options in the last nearly thirty years that would have required me to pause, be honest with myself about the situation, and make an intentional decision to have a conversation, not deliver a message. What if I had told her what I was experiencing and asked her how it was going for her? What if I had not held onto what I thought leadership looked like and, as her "superior," leveraged a decision about her rather than with her? The outcome *might* have been the same, but how she experienced me would have been in line with who I wanted to be, and that is *not* the experience she had. There was a moment to *pause* and play out the impact and how it would align to my brand. I missed the moment.

The courageous and insightful Viktor Frankl has been credited saying, "Between stimulus and response, there is a space. In that space lies our freedom and our power to choose our response. In our response lies our growth and our happiness" (Baker 2018). This space is where the power is to show up authentically, intentionally, with a lens to what people will know you for, aligned to your values, and consistent to how you want people to feel because of your actions and words.

Prior to his role as an education leader in a large school district, Joe Fabey invested in students in the classroom as a teacher. Early in his career, he was the beloved teacher in the second-grade classroom and had a student who we'll call James. James advanced through elementary school and graduated onto junior high, then high school. He then matriculated to United States Military Academy AT West Point. Joe lost touch with James and his family but was aware of his success beyond his time in Mr. Fabey's second grade classroom.

Fabey also progressed in that time, moving out of the classroom and into educational administration. In his natural connecting-with-people state, Fabey was talking with the principal at one of his elementary schools. The principal mentioned hiring a new fifth grade teacher and a fantastic candidate they had found from across the country. The first and last name of the star candidate was shared and caught Fabey's attention. Drawing on his curiosity, Joe told the principal to ask the new hire if her husband's name was "James." Sure enough, the new fifth grade teacher was in fact married to James and Fabey had sniffed it out. This was the James from Fabey's second grade classroom twenty years earlier. James was returning to the area to take a command at the army base, which is why his wife was looking for a job.

The reunion between Mr. Fabey and James was the opening for James to share that he never forgot his second grade teacher. As was common at the time, many households had a code word that meant the parent needed to make it easy for the kid to get out of a situation—for instance, sleeping over at a friend's house and being homesick. These words were chosen based on common knowledge in the family, like something easy to remember and easily relatable. Sometimes words are made up of the first initial of each member of the family; sometimes it is a word that is easy to use in a sentence. In fact, James's family had used "Fabey" as their code word, a nod to the inclusive environment Mr. Fabey created for his students and their families. Somehow, he was showing up as a young second grade teacher, instilling his values to connect with kids in a way they are still talking about him as a model twenty years later.

Models come in all forms and at any point in our lives and our careers. With a deep tech expertise who now leverages that to advise boards and consult in the tech space, Pravin Raj credits his early days at Cisco Systems when he had an unsuspecting place to learn the impact of showing up. In late 2000, Raj was part of the sales team in Texas that hosted John Chambers, CEO of Cisco Systems, for twenty-four hours. The time they spent with customers and dining with colleagues, Chambers remembered each person's name. He greeted them and knew each person regardless of the size of the team.

While that was notable, what was remarkable was taking Chambers to the airport at the end of their twenty-four hours together. Raj took his CEO to the airport. He accompanied him inside with his large hanging bag. Raj suggested Chambers check the bag given the size and length. Chambers told him he was flying to Orlando, and immediately upon landing he would be on his way to a black-tie affair. This long bag contained his tuxedo for him to change into, alleviating the time pressure of waiting at baggage claim and delaying his arrival at the event. Raj did not question the justification and took the bag to the X-ray machine that was more of a size checker than anything. This was before 9/11, when airports did not have security lines and extensive screenings. While Raj was waiting for his CEO's bag to run through the machine, said CEO was greeting each security guard by shaking their hand and thanking them for what they do. Raj noticed how Chambers interacted and connected with people, and it was not in a salesy way. There was not anything he was trying to get out of the other person. He was merely showing up, demonstrating respect and integrity to each person—no different than how Raj had felt in his presence. The impact was so profound, Raj was left feeling he would walk to the end of the world for that man just because of how he treated him in that twenty-four-hour period.

You don't have to have it figured out early in your career or in your life, but there are steps to take and pivots to make on your journey. While this chapter highlights stories of career and positional managers, leadership is a capability and is offered to all of us in all situations. Family roles and dynamics arguably are the earliest and biggest playing field we encounter this chance. For those thrust into a blended family, defining how you show up is low on the priority list amidst the new found love of your partner and, hopefully, the kids. The moments can seem fleeting. They may seem small or insignificant. But when overlooked they build your brand. And without clarity and definition, that brand might not be what you want out in the world as identifiers of you. The time or energy to pause and deliberately move through them may seem big—but the investment and focus will deliver dividends demonstrating who you are. More importantly, the moments you don't overlook but pause and purposefully respond to will reconcile how you show up in this world. You can be aligned to your true self and be rewarded for the connection you experience with others. As for the failures, you will not have failed on being true to your authentic self, making the learning academic and not about your character.

PAUSE FOR PRACTICE

Here is where the "Pause" pages mentioned in the introduction begin. Each chapter will end with some practice prompts. The pages that follow are intentionally left blank · to serve as a reminder to slow down and reflect.

- ► Begin with a reflection of a leader you admire and identify what you believe to be their core values. What actions have you observed that indicate those values?
- ► Core values are your belief system—how you measure right and wrong; how you go about the world. A few examples are honesty, integrity, kindness, and courage. Take the time to be still and do a deep reflection. From the list of values that follow, capture your top ten. Do not overthink it. Just circle the ones that jump out to you first. Then narrow that list to five. Then identify your top three—and capture them on the following page to refer to throughout the book.
- ► Reflect on when you have shown up consistent with your values. What indicators did others observe in support of that? What is a time you did not act or show up aligned to your core values? What got in your way? If you could do it differently, what would you do?

Acceptance
Accountability
Accuracy
Achievement
Adaptability
Adventure
Aesthetics
Agility
Altruism
Ambition
Assertiveness
Authenticity
Authority
Autonomy
Balance
Beauty
Being
Belonging
Boldness
Camaraderie
Candor
Challenge
Citizenship
Collaboration
Comfort
Commitment
Community
Compassion
Competence
Confidence
Connection
Consistency

Contentment
Contribution
Convention
Cooperation
Courage
Creativity
Curiosity
Decisiveness
Dependability
Determination
Dignity
Diligence
Diversity
Drive
Duty
Ecology
Efficiency
Environment
Equality
Ethics
Excellence
Expertise
Fairness
Faith
Fame
Family
Financial
Flexibility
Focus
Forgiveness
Freedom
Friendship

Fun
Generosity
Genuineness
Grace
Gratitude
Growth
Happiness
Harmony
Health
Helpfulness
Honesty
Hope
Humility
Humor
Inclusion
Independence
Influence
Inner harmony
Innovative
Integrity
Intuitiveness
Justice
Kindness
Knowledge
Leadership
Learning
Legacy
Leisure
Likability
Love
Loyalty
Meaningful work

Moderation
Nature
Openness
Optimism
Order
Originality
Parenting
Passion
Patience
Patriotism
Peace
Perseverance
Pleasure
Poise
Popularity
Power
Pragmatism
Pride
Privacy
Proactivity

Professionalism
Recognition
Reliability
Religion
Reputation
Resourcefulness
Respect
Responsibility
Risk-taking
Security
Self-discipline
Self-expression
Self-respect
Serenity
Service
Simplicity
Solitude
Sophistication
Speed
Spirituality

Sportsmanship
Stability
Status
Stewardship
Success
Teamwork
Time
Tradition
Travel
Trust
Understanding
Uniqueness
Usefulness
Variety
Vision
Vulnerability
Wealth
Wellness
Wholeheartedness
Wisdom

(If you do not see a value that is core to you, add it here.)

*Note: this list is compiled from the many that exist. It is not exhaustive.

PAUSE FOR PRACTICE PAGE

PAUSE FOR PRACTICE PAGE

Pause for Language

"The difference between the almost right word and the right word is really a large matter—it's the difference between the lightning bug and the lightning."

—MARK TWAIN

AMERICAN WRITER AND HUMORIST

Several months into my relationship with Jeff, we were in the flurry of activity that four kids bring, navigating homework, basketball practice, violin lessons, and the liveliness that goes along with it all. Still trying to get our arms around how to calm the chaos and make some semblance of a schedule, we took inventory with the kids about their priorities, plans, and expectations of the next few days. The chirps of going to a movie with my friends, the football game with so and so, and can I have a sleep over were commonplace, and Scott piped in about an activity with "my mom." We kept the flow going and managed to get to a point of victory of having some skeleton of a plan for the next several days and patting ourselves on the backs that all kids were getting to and from and with all their "things."

When the kids were gone and we had time to catch our breath and connect and discuss how getting to this point went, Jeff shared what was troubling to him. The fluidity of houses between Jeff and the mom of his kids was fairly easy at that point, so that was not alarming. What caught him off guard was his son's possessive pronoun of "my mom" versus the familiar reference that she was just "mom." He shared that he could remember when his parents divorced, and he started talking about the other parent as "my" instead of the common role of dad or mom to the nuclear family.

Personal pronouns—I, my, you, theirs, they—are more powerful than the unintended omission implies. They identify who we are talking about or to, and they can create a connection between the parties. The small insertion of what James Pennebaker refers to as invisible stealth words in *The Secret Life of Pronouns* has a far greater impact than a two-letter word might indicate. The power of these qualifiers signal confidence, connection, power, unity, and many other things. If and when overlooked, they can relay an unintentional message (Pennebaker 2011).

The impact of these words surface in everyday conversation, facilitation in group settings, even ordering at a restaurant. While recently out to dinner with Ellie, the server greeted us and asked, "Do we know what we want to drink?"

We placed our drink orders, and as the server left I shared my frustration how this person is not part of "we." They are not having a drink with us, they are not part of the action we are enjoying, and inserting themselves as part of the experience when they are not I find off-putting. Ellie shared a completely different perspective—that it was very inclusive and delivered a feeling of commitment the server is invested in our dining experience, and the "we" signaled that. The enlightened generation I mentioned in the Introduction can be heard in this experience as well as the difference in language use and interpretation. We had two contrasting reactions to the simple use of a two letter word in the same situation. Expressing explicit clarity of intent and word choice becomes paramount.

When facilitating any type of group discussion or training, we often start with norms and expectations to create a brave learning environment. We set the stage with agreements for the optimal engagement and least unintentional disconnect. Along with active listening, assuming good intent, and being fully present, we purposefully use "I" language. Using "I" language signals to our coworkers that we own our statements, our positions, and our sharing. Without this cue, we can easily slip into speaking in the third person or in more general terms. The further we get from owning our position, the more dangerous our statements can become detached from our beliefs, experiences, or ideas.

July 4, 2006, Jeff and I married in a historic chapel on Jekyll Island, Georgia. In that little chapel with original Tiffany stained glass windows, Ellie was dropping flower petals as the real time flower girl and the escort of the bride as we walked to meet Jeff and his three kids at the altar. We exchanged vows and said, "I do," and included the kids with symbols of connection when we exchanged our rings. Our words were intentional. "I do" is what we committed. Wedding vows have evolved. Sometimes they are from the church and very traditional, while some are very personal and more narrative. But they all signal a personal promise and begin with "I."

Imagine the implied "I" so often absent in professional situations in the wedding vows: "Do you Megan, take this man…" and my reply was, "Do." Think about how often you have been on the delivering or receiving end of that subtle omission of the word signaling ownership of the emotion, commitment, or connection.

Think about the last time you were professionally acknowledged for your contributions. The audience who witnessed this acknowledgement is one element of this equation, and the word choice is arguably more important. Did they say, "Appreciate your hard work," or did they say, "I appreciate your hard work"? The distinction is minor, or the language shift could be even greater to something like, "I appreciate the amount of time and detail you put into the final client deck." Let's look at the nuance of "appreciate" versus "I appreciate." The "I" is assumed, yet when we use "I," it indicates emotional awareness and connection from the person speaking the gratitude. The absence of "I" can also be heard as a directive—"you should appreciate your work"—which changes the message entirely to one of acknowledgement from someone else to direction of how you should be feeling. Omitting the qualifier creates distance, and using a different qualifier can create possessiveness. Consider how Scott's use of "my mom" established a division in the former nuclear family and served as a stark reminder of the shift in family systems.

How we talk about others when we talk to them and when we talk about them can deliver a message separate from what is actually communicated. The possessive versus inclusive nature of pronouns seems to be a fine line when a manager refers to "my team" instead of "our team." Language, specifically pronouns, signals the speaker's emotional health as well as their confidence and can create feelings of belonging, which increase inclusion and confidence. When this is lacking and leaders feel more isolated, so does the use of inward focusing first-person singular pronouns like "I" and "me" (Burkus 2015). This can be experienced as posturing, claiming others' positions and contributions as those of the manager and diminishing the individual experience to the receiving audience. To the leader it can be a much needed signal they are not serving themselves in the approach they are taking to serve others.

While I was a pharmaceutical representative, our beloved district manager often communicated to us that when we succeeded it was the team contributions, and when we missed (or failed) it was on him as the district manager. This leader's acknowledgment about our efforts and hard work created a sense of belonging, a desire to strive, and a motivation to win in the marketplace. As a hard-working team member, I saw myself in the team, the collective effort requiring my contributions, and how success would be shared and acknowledged. The language was void of ego and showboating. Instead it established cohesiveness, in it together-ness, and the base line for establishing psychological safety to ask for help without fear.

Having worked with managers who refer to "my team" or make commitments for "my team to do that," I have seen how it can certainly draw speculation of capability and desire of those on the team and questions of whether a task will be pushed down to someone in service of the ego and posturing of the manager. The manager who inserts in a peer-level meeting saying "My team can do that" can suggest that person will turn around and task someone with what they just signed up to do. "We can do that" signals collaboration or a skillset on the team that exists or can develop.

The possessive pronoun "my" generates a feeling of division. It's one or the other; ownership not inclusion. The deliberate insertion of personal and possessive pronouns are a distinction of bringing people together, identifying place of belonging. When overlooked or defaulted, it can quickly disenfranchise the very group you are striving to empower and ignite. Through the use of first-person plural pronouns and second person pronouns, leaders are seen as more effective and avoid use of first-person pronouns referencing themselves, according to research from organizational experts Rasmus Hougaard and Jaqueline Carter (2018). Often overlooked and hard to decipher in language is how a leader sees themself belonging in the company or team.

We communicate to others how we see ourselves in systems, organizations, and families. Jeff and I collectively brought four kids to our marriage. *His* three from his previous marriage and *my* one from my previous marriage became *our* four kids. Through a long and physically and emotionally hard road, which we will not cover in this book, Jeff adopted my one. She became our kid, and we still have four kids. The distinction in ours is not possessive in nature but inclusive of the family we created in our union. Yet when people, and even those very close to us, ask how we are doing, they check in on Ellie and inevitably look to Jeff and say, "And how are *your* kids, Jeff?" Our deliberate choice of language to signal belonging, which we will talk more about in "Pause to Belonging," is challenged with the message we fail to deliver. The distinction others make *to* us signaling whose kids they see them as stings. Listening to how others talk about themselves, and aping that, indicates recognition of expressed and communication preferences.

There are several levels of listening, from background noise to fully focused hearing body language, tone, breath, and words. When we truly listen to others, we can pick up on nuance, subtle distinctions in tone and breath, and body language that deliver broader messages. We will talk more about this in "Pause for Connection" with the bait and bobber approach, but it is worth noting that listening is a key component to language. When we really hear what someone is telling us, we choose language to respond that creates connection, not a bigger gap.

Kyle Samuel is an insurance executive and carries what he learned at the Leading with Character and Competence program at West Point. Military leaders teach the programmatic elements in the course. One of the pillars of leadership that resonates with Kyle is that clarity of the mission in the military can mean life or death. In the corporate world it can mean success or failure. So as the leader, your primary responsibility is to ensure people understand the mission. The framing this leader used is, "I don't know what I said until you tell me what you heard." We think we are clear, and we are quick to deliver messages, but sometimes we fail to check and make sure our teams and our leaders understood what was intended. Clarify the message delivered is the same as the message received.

A CEO recently told me how important it is to connect with the people in his organization, both one-on-one and in small groups. He talks to them about their work, what's going on in their lives, and what he's been up to. This type of informal talk increases connection and trust between him and his employees. The diverse representation in the company wants to know him as a person, and they want to know they are seen and heard by him. However, he shared that he does not add his pronouns to his Zoom name because he is old school, and that action doesn't fit him. The research is widely known that pronouns increase belonging, and accurate pronouns make us feel seen (Johnson et al. 2021). Gender pronouns are one of the easiest ways to generate belonging. This is one of those seemingly benign moments overlooked by leaders that we referred to in the introduction as adding up in significance. Even though he acknowledges the importance of one-on-one meetings and seeing individuals, he sends a different message with his default to "old school," and by *not* adding pronouns to his signature demonstrates an intentional choice of *what* others experience of him

Inserting words, or silence, or omitting words serve as an impact that can establish power. Selectively choosing to omit pronouns, to add them, to clarify, to add articles, or assume common understanding by omitting are intentional choices that signal significance to the recipient of the message.

Clearly deciding the impact you intend to deliver requires choosing words—even the little ones—to align to your intent. The lack of words can create a boundary as easily as the lack of words or silence can be used to pull people in rather than shutting them down. Each of these nuanced decisions will signal and impress a brand about you. This is often another overlooked opportunity to pause and choose intentionally the impact you establish.

My first work-related public speaking event was addressing an eager group of college alumni during a reunion planning weekend. Some of the alums knew each other from college; some were familiar from volunteering over the years; others did not have as many acquaintances but had the alma mater and other interests in common. This made for a lot of side conversations and chatter. When it was time for me to speak, I went to the podium, noticed my youth to their experience, and simply waited. The modeling I had seen was to ask for attention, request people to quiet and take their seats, or to tap something to make a noise that might draw attention and signal a transition in the room. What I chose was to simply observe and hold my space. The time it took for the room to quiet was remarkably faster than the other approaches.

Silence is an approach to get attention of a crowd. It is also an effective approach to invite others to speak more. A tactic used by litigation attorneys, teachers, parents and others is to ask a question and wait. People will respond, but when you wait a bit longer before interjecting, signals you are listening and is an invitation for the other person to continue to share. Another technique is to notice how much you are speaking and restrain until three other voices have been heard before sharing, or ask yourself why am I talking (WAIT) to force the pause and connect to your intent. And when you speak again, what words will you use?

Words are the most common way to quickly convey your brand and values. When used without intention, they can deliver a powerful and misaligned impact. Elton Ndoma-Ogar, expert diversity and inclusion practitioner and leader, played college football. His role model was awe-inspiring coach Jim Caldwell. Caldwell joined Wake Forest University during Elton's tenure there. Caldwell had an impressive track record of success in collegiate football coaching and as the first African American head coach in the Atlantic Coach Conference. Ndoma-Ogar recalls that his presence was distinctive in that he didn't raise his voice or use profanity, and he talked about being well-read, well-spoken, well-dressed, well-mannered, and well-traveled. He poured this into everyone he came around.

Caldwell empowered his team to vote for their captain. Elton was unanimously voted captain by all of his teammates during Coach Caldwell's first year as coach and Elton's first year as a player (after a red shirt year). Coach Caldwell met Elton's self-admitted cocky arrogance and enthusiasm to be captain with expectations by telling him he would not be representing his team as the captain. He saw more in Elton than his posturing and attitude.

The next year, Elton's teammates voted for him again. Elton strutted into Coach Caldwell's office with his starting games roster and support of his teammates as indicators of his skill and position yet failed to take inventory of Coach Caldwell's vote. Again, Coach Caldwell suggested looking at the data of how Elton communicated. He shared examples of Elton's use of profanity, citing how as intelligent as Elton was he could find a more effective way to communicate his message. Remember, Caldwell's mantra was to be well-read, well-*spoken*, well-dressed, well-mannered, and well-traveled. He was failing to hear Ndoma-Ogar as well-spoken, and that impact compromised his ability to show up as any of the other criteria because it is a package, a presence.

This time, when Caldwell voted in opposition to the teams' vote for captain, Elton took notice. That was 1994. Elton has not used another curse word since that moment. And he became captain the following year.

Contrary to his offensive lineman stature and presence, Elton mimics Coach Caldwell by not raising his voice, not using profanity, and holding a place to contribute to conversations through curiosity and a calm demeanor. Whether it is meeting with colleagues, on a call with people junior to him, or in a higher visibility and level setting, he asks thoughtful questions to bring others in—like favorite books, movies, sitcoms, or albums. And he waits for others to answer. And he listens to the response. When facilitating a large group where engagement can be slow to come and people can be timid to speak or join in, he uses words to communicate he is comfortable in the silence to allow them to join when they are ready. He then leverages the silence for others to find their way to engage in the dialogue.

Having intentional word choice, knowing your audience, knowing yourself, and knowing how you want to show up, listen, and be perceived give space for our ability to connect and belong. What is the process you deploy to choose words, language, audience, and desired impact? When preparing before a meeting—with your kid's teacher, your boss, your mentor, your kids, your parents, your colleague… anyone, really—determine how you want to show up and how you want to feel and be felt at the end of that interaction. How do others describe your language and communication style? Does it draw others in, or do you trend more toward taking up all the air in the room?

PAUSE FOR PRACTICE

- ▶ When we are present, we actively listen. We pick up on the cues others offer us—a terse "fine" in response to "How are you doing?" signals the person is not in fact "fine." Being present to connect to what you want to convey takes focus and an increased awareness so that when the split moments arise you are more readily connected to that message you want to convey.
  - Notice who you have a more challenging time connecting with. What is nuanced about your language when you communicate with them or when they communicate with you?
  - Notice what might it be signaling to you and what words you are omitting or using that might make a difference.
- ▶ Sometimes language is the key. Sometimes silence has a greater impact. Where can you establish a greater connection by holding space for a pause—or no response? Use the acronym WAIT—why am I

talking—to help discern when you can offer the space to someone else.

▶ What pronouns do you tend to use when speaking to your team? Your family? Your family about your workmates? How are you talking about people when you speak *to* them, and is that different from how you speak *about* them?

PAUSE FOR PRACTICE PAGE

PAUSE FOR PRACTICE PAGE

Pause for Clarity

"If your actions inspire others to dream more, learn more, do more and become more, you are a leader."

—JOHN QUINCY ADAMS

SIXTH PRESIDENT TO THE UNITED STATES OF AMERICA (1825–1829)

One night, as our two-year-old slept soundly in her crib, I was fast asleep having grown tired watching *Tin Cup* with my then-husband. But I knew my daughter's morning would come early and that I had best be ready for it. I woke to the room alit with every light shining with a story to tell, the closet door figuratively and literally opening and closing, and the squeak of hardwood floors holding in nearly one hundred years of secrets and stories. He returned the room, and me, back to darkness before crawling into bed telling me he did not think I loved him anymore. The sound of his voice was startling, but his words were unsympathetic. Our marriage was harder than I thought it would be, and I had lost myself in the commitment to it. After a year of intentionally working to find myself again, he noticed but misnamed what was happening. When I shared I had been focusing on me, and

I quit leading the band and the music stopped, he replied with his truth. His truth was that he had been unfaithful in the duration of our relationship and was, in his words, struggling with homosexuality. This was followed with a bid to go to marital counseling, which we had already done, and an offer to divorce.

The spotlight was shining on the clarity I had on that dark stage, and I was ready to play the role I was cast into. We had a daughter whom I loved dearly, and I was not willing to model an unhealthy relationship for her, so I stated my certainty: "We will be getting divorced, but there is a right way and a wrong way to go about this. We have a long time to co-parent together, and we will do this the right way." I made the decision, with precision, in the moment that it mattered. Not all decisions are this obvious. Either they are not offered so clearly or our response is not so clear. But this one was, and I embraced it for what was right and who I was and how this aligned to both.

While the moment was the most transparent instant of our marriage, it was riddled with conflict. Conflict, by definition, is a competitive or opposing action of incompatibles. Divorce is an obvious depiction of that incompatibility, yet conflict presents far more often than accredited. Conflict arises when there are differing beliefs, needs, wants, understandings, values, truths, and so on. When conflict surfaces, it creates energy and a need to decide how to engage.

Doctors Thomas and Kilmann developed a model of different conflict styles that is based on two underlying dimensions of human behavior: assertiveness and cooperativeness.

Assertiveness is when we prioritize our own concerns, whereas cooperativeness prioritizes the other person's concerns. Depending on the degree to which we engage in the conflict, putting a higher priority on one axis over the other, there are five defined styles of conflict engagement:

- ▸ Avoidance, which neither pursues one's own concerns or those of another;
- ▸ Accommodating, which indexes higher on the other person's concerns and neglects one's own;
- ▸ Collaborating, which works to find a mutual solution;
- ▸ Competing, which prioritizes one's own priority at the expense of the other's; and
- ▸ Compromising, which often is the quick exit out of the conflict (1974).

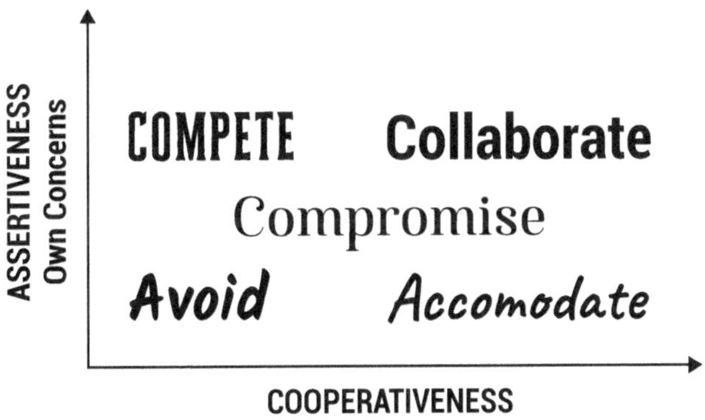

I leaned into a compromising approach because it sounded like the path of least resistance based on the information I had at the time. It was the middle ground of concern for others and concern for self. While I would love to say the divorce process and years that followed were so clear and amicable, that is not the case, and I had lots of practice time in each of the quadrants trying on different conflict styles. Dialing in from "Pause to Show Up," getting clarity on how you want others to see and feel your presence is a key contributor to the conflict style you *choose*, which others can easily hijack without your awareness.

Flying from her home state of North Carolina to New York City to welcome a newly acquired managing director and team, Susan, chief human resources officer for the division, was looking forward to meeting her new colleagues. She was prepared to work with this new executive, bringing her expertise of the people side of the business along with deep institutional knowledge of how to get things done. She met the slick industry business line leaders who were to be her new partners. The Park Avenue introductions swiftly shifted to questions with a twang of judgment. "What can you possibly do for me?" slyly referenced her soft southern accent and the five hundred miles between the epicenter of any New Yorker and her career home office in North Carolina.

Susan quickly (even by New York standards) replied that while the inquirer knew *his* business, *she* knew the people and the institution he now worked for. She went on to say if he wanted to get anything done and needed people to do it, he would not be able to accomplish it without her. Now she had his attention through the demonstration of her value rather than an engagement in conflict. She quickly aligned to her brand of being a resource, not an adversary. They did become partners and succeeded, but it took intentional work.

The accomplishments of the business were significant, and their friendship and respect even more so.

Early in her career years, former Procter & Gamble executive, Emily K., had an adversarial colleague who created an environment of conflict on a key team where they were expected to partner. The scenario drained Emily, and she called in "the big guns" to come to the meeting and lay down the law. The senior leader she invited readily agreed to join. The meeting started, and this colleague demonstrated all the behaviors Emily experienced as conflict-ridden. She positioned herself at the table, comfortably ready to watch this colleague get put in his place. What she witnessed instead was this superior, with the power to shut it down, engage in diffusing the conflict through inquiry and ask questions to uncover the person's values, to gain an understanding of what was in it for them, and to uncover what was driving their approach. This conflict style of moving along the cooperativeness axis—putting the other person's concern first or at least *in* the discussion—quickly reduced the tension and shed light on what was happening.

This superior, who had the organizational power to enter in and leverage a decision, placed a higher value on understanding the goal than the goal itself. It was felt not as much a conflict style but a diffusion style. This approach opened a dialogue and moved the conflicting parties in a direction that created good will and positive outcomes. As a professional who built her career in design—creating brands, understanding the user, targeting the right customer with the right branding and innovation—Emily had missed it with her colleague. But when she called in the senior leader to control the situation in her favor, she learned a new and scalable approach.

The boss's boss of early career project manager Randy Lyons summoned him to a meeting. The collective of managers was questioning the project he was running and were doubting the estimated time he calculated. Refraining from inquiry of details about the work, the higher ups communicated a commitment to a shorter timeline. Describing a clear breakdown of the detail and the options and alternatives, Randy showed exhausted pathways to support why the shortened timeline commitment was not feasible.

Had the higher ups drilled into the details, they would learn the team had engaged in many iterations, and iterating on the iterations, to try and bring the timing down. They had invested their personal time and compromised their priorities with family, plans, vacations and balance around their work and life in commitment to the mission. Randy led them through informed estimating and building in contingency for the "unknown unknowns" that always happen in projects like these, including new capabilities and technology for the company.

The collection of bosses was telling Randy if he could not do it on the shortened timeline they would leverage their positional power to find someone who could. Randy knew his team feared being marched into failure and that he would be strongarmed into committing them to something based on less than data and planning. Knowing this and unwilling to demonstrate to his team he would sign them up for something that would compromise their integrity and boundaries, Randy was willing to risk his job for them and the success of the project. He told them if they could find someone to do what they had committed to deliver in the compressed time frame then to please do so. The work was going to take every bit of the longer timeline, and if there was someone who can do it faster he would like to learn from them.

Following him out, his manager and that manager's manager instructed him to go back in and commit to the shorter timeframe. Randy held true to his position that without additional resources the work will take as long as he committed, and he was not going to say he would do something the team and he could not deliver. Fully expecting to be fired, he stood his ground with his clarity of integrity aligned to his values. He was not fired, nor was he taken off the project. He delivered it to the timeline he estimated, fully representing his brand.

The deliverable was successful. The output was what was asked and needed. Randy did take a hit from the senior executive in his evaluation period in his performance rating. But Randy was clear this was due to a misalignment of the senior exec not understanding the work and consulting with who was responsible for delivering it before committing to deadlines. Randy had to work alongside this exec for years to come. He managed the relationship but lacked respect for the opaque behavior—the exec was protecting his own reputation versus setting others up for success. Randy used that manager and his behavior as his gauge to determine how people he was leading felt based on his actions as their leader to ensure he did not call in to question the integrity of the individuals on his teams as he had been.

The energy that arises from conflict will often trigger a reaction or a response, and that response is a moment of power to unlock great connection, establish rapport, build trust, shift perspective, and many other possible positive results *if* you are clear in your values and how you want to be experienced by others. This is an intentional moment to notice what the conflict is about, leverage your curiosity to explore what is driving the conflict, and then choosing the action.

There were many, many, many times in trying to blend our family of six when I was inverted in representing whose concern I was prioritizing. With enough fraught engagements, I became more aware in the moment of what approach I was taking and more intentional, but I would be crazy to imply I came close to figuring that out in the formative years when all three of my stepkids were still home!

The old adage goes, "Is it more important to be right, or to get along?" There are times in organizations that the data matters and the outcome caries significance, and those are the times to lean into the higher priority of the goal to influence your intentional choice of conflict style. Other times it is more heavily weighted toward relationships—for other people to have their voices heard or to try something knowing it will fail to establish a learning environment. Be present with yourself to know the difference and align to the axis most valuable in the situation.

PAUSE FOR PRACTICE

- ► When conflict arises, name the higher priority—goal or relationship. Be able to clarify what makes the relationship or goal important and proceed with the style that will continue to align with that outcome.
  - ◆ Reflect back on your values you capture in "Pause to Show Up." What does your approach to conflict demonstrate about your values, and how clear are they to others?
- ► Is it more important to be right or to get along? It is an old saying, but the saying offers truth.
  - ◆ What is the purpose of the conflict and the engagement?
  - ◆ Are you looking to establish power?
  - ◆ If so, is it necessary?
  - ◆ What makes this the place to establish it.
  - ◆ If not, what is another approach to take?
- ► Reflect on how you would like others to perceive you in conflict when you're fully aligned to your brand.
  - ◆ Who observes you and is courageous enough to share what it is like to be on the other side of a conflict with you?
  - ◆ Ask them and be open to what they say. Is this consistent with how you want to be experienced?
  - ◆ If not, how can you shift in that direction?
  - ◆ If yes, what might get in the way of consistently showing up aligned to your brand in times of disagreement?

PAUSE FOR PRACTICE PAGE

PAUSE FOR PRACTICE PAGE

Pause to Connect

"We don't accomplish anything in this world alone… and whatever happens is the result of the whole tapestry of one's life and all the weavings of individual threads from one to another that creates something."

—SANDRA DAY O'CONNOR

FIRST FEMALE ASSOCIATE JUSTICE OF THE

SUPREME COURT OF THE UNITED STATES

We pulled up to the faded blue house that sat across from the park on the cul-de-sac. When Jeff put the car in park on the steep driveway, we sat in silence. The front door was hard to find. It tucked around a corner with a landscape boulder in front of the sidewalk, blocking an easy entrance, and I knew that what lived behind that door was oxygen deprived: the primer painted bathroom; the wood floors baring the stories of families navigating rites of passage and coming of age; carpets holding the remnants of puppies growing to dogs and kittens to cats and all that leaves behind; windows not able to hold their own weight and screwed shut; and furniture showing worn effects of a too harsh sun and torn from rough housing with window cranks on leaky windows and rambunctious kids. This man I loved lived in this house. And we were at a point to decide where to live with our combined four kids.

This house seemed the obvious choice of two since it had the space for all of our kids, which my high-on-curb-appeal home did not. Other reasons sided in favor of the house for the least change with the majority of the kids and the higher ages. If we were balancing a scale, the chips would fall in their favor. But the real issue I identified was, "The problem is that I consider this house a complete fixer upper, and you are completely comfortable living in it as is." It sounded so much sharper than I had intended when the words came out, yet I put words to thoughts and he preferred the less vocal approach, though he audibly agreed this was, in fact, true. He is not one to shy from conversations that have depth, but it takes me tossing the line with bait to get him to bite.

I began referencing this as the bait and bobber approach to communication and connection based on fishing references. The bait is what you put on a fishing-line hook and cast into the water to get the fish to bite, set the hook, and then reel them in. Bait is under the surface. Bobbers sit on top of the water; in fact, they often are what keep the bait from going *too* deep under the water. When someone in the office asks how you are, do you answer with brevity with one or two words— like "fine" or "well"—and in the neutral to positive? That is the bobber approach. Or do you answer with something a little more substantive—"Things are pretty good, but there have been some hard things lately," or "Things are going great, and I am finding a lot of balance with meaningful work and time with my family"—a response that goes deeper and opens up a relatability to others. These moments are so easy to capture and absorb yet are often overlooked to finish just one email; to show as "green" on Microsoft Teams; to appear as engaged as your level of effort implies. Yet your engagement wanes because of your decision to *appear* engaged.

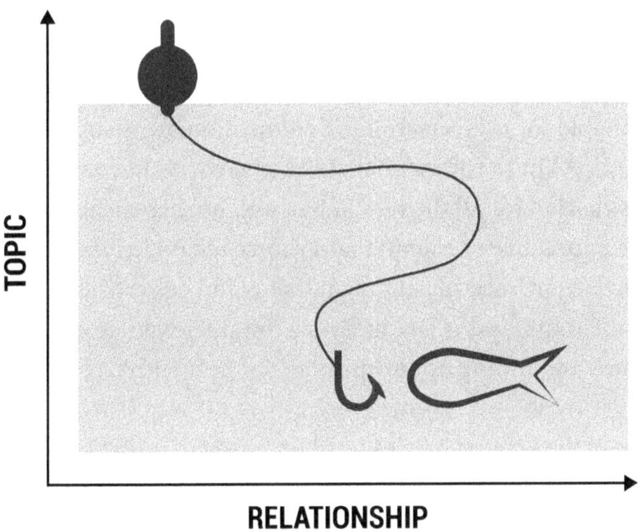

The awareness of the opportunities to connect are often overlooked in the hurried nature of what is already in motion—you are in the middle of writing an email, someone stops by, or your child walks in your office—and the nature to stay focused or prioritize what you are already doing wins the competition for your attention. The awareness this is happening is often overlooked, and these are the opportunities that signal our priorities, yet we often fail to recognize them.

The conflict styles diagram from "Pause for Clarity" maps concern for self against concern for others as the intersection of where the different approaches come into play. The bait and bobber approach to connection has a similar mapping with a slightly different definition of the axis. Connection is determined by the relationship versus the topic. A bait connection will lean heavily into listening and asking and seeking to hear and to be heard. This approach prioritizes the relationship or connection with the person. At its deepest level it is agnostic of the topic or issue. A bobber interaction will skate along the surface regardless of who or what is available for conversation or connection at its superficial depth. Akin to the conflict styles, there is a time and place or situation for all degrees of bait and bobber engagements. It is a measure of intentionality to check ourselves in how much we are meeting our own desires and needs to authentic connection, and it is a measure to take inventory of how others are finding opportunity to connect with us.

One of the greatest bait leaders I have seen in action traversed the halls of the city center high rise, looking for interactions while waiting for the elevator, ordering in the building café, or hurriedly walking past the divisions of cubicles and work spaces to arrive at his office. Regardless of the number of people waiting for his next meeting or time left to be on his next call, he neglected to give off the rushed-to-something-more-important feel to those at all levels beneath his title. He maximized the art of being present, casting and hooking the bait of the pleasantries, offering more than the platitudes of "how are you" and "fine," leaving others to flop on the dock like a fish out of water. In his wake his employees engaged with their work and the mission of the organization and felt connected to someone from the ivory towers because he saw them and created connection, even in the smallest of time spans. And he could feel a connection *to* them, not just one he was providing *for* others.

This leader stepped into a higher level C suite position, taking his bait approach to a smaller and more start-up like environment with more locations and fewer employees than the hustle and bustle of the vibrant city skyscraper he left. While the new job was not in an industry worlds apart, the personalities of the individuals and their values were definitively more defined and expressed. While he was able to move about his day in his former role and spend less time for a deep impact, his new position commanded more depth from him than he previously delivered. The new employee base craves more than trusting the head honcho is leading the company in the right direction. These disciples of the organization want to *know* him, they want access to him, and they want him to stop and talk and, more important, to listen and hear them. And they want evidence he hears them. Mission and values drive them. They demonstrate their priorities in the artifacts they decorate their workspace with, the causes they represent on their T-shirts, and the events they attend together as colleagues and friends. They want to know mission and values drive him, too, and they want to know what those are from spending time with him. His days include spending time in the hallways, engaging in bait conversations that both go deep and are marked by time. His days of walking through the halls and having bait interactions in smaller time increments are not the same measure of value in his new role. He has a choice of where he indexes on the two axis. The connection he feels and how he intends to have an impact is on the relationship axis, going deep in the waters and swimming after the bait.

The choice we each encounter is how we anticipate the actual and proverbial hallway chats. Walking through hallways with blinders on and a focus for the destination to where you are heading, averting eyes in the event someone were to actually speak up and attempt to get your attention, creates an experience *of* you *to* them. This is a bobber approach, avoiding the discussion, tossing out pleasantries like candy off a float at a parade and keeping the pace. Swimming toward the intentional bait end of the connection pool is to engage in these conversations at a focused level, thinking about how you want the other person to *feel* from time spent with you and focusing on what you will *learn* about them and what you will share about you.

One of my favorite leaders I have had the pleasure to work with would walk through the office and stop to speak with me. He would look at me, ask questions, and offer input to the conversation—a true dialogue. He looked for the connection points of what or who we had in common and would follow up on these tidbits we shared when we would see each other again many months later. I sat in an open desk area, and he did the same thing with each of us, not just me, signaling a consistent part of who he is, not just a shared connection with one or two people. His smile as he approached and slowed his pace signaled it came from a place of his belonging and not just leading the organization, creating a place for us to belong.

In 1989, when Dave O'Callaghan (DOC) joined the Ford Motor Company, he observed the incoming quality supervisor focus on relationships. This man named Bernie knew *everyone*. He focused on the relationships, invested in knowing people. He spent his time walking the plant floor to establish his presence and receive the presence of others. If something was going on with someone, he knew about it because he made it his business to know the people. The modeling of this approach imprinted on DOC, and he adopted this way of establishing and assessing credibility in an organization.

Now as a consultant, DOC still utilizes this approach to knowing everyone in the field all the way to the CEO. He asks questions and for opinions and listens to the responses. He listens to hear and to learn what that tells him about the person. He follows through with what he says he is going to do, and he shows up to share about himself too. This sounds easy. It sounds like DOC has a cush job with no stress, and he can walk around all day chatting people up and shooting the breeze—quite the contrary. DOC gets thrust into situations where plants are underperforming and people are at risk of losing their jobs, or, worse, the quality of the problems impacts safety and lives of people on the job using the end products of what these plants are creating. This approach to connection has steered him through some hard situations when he has made difficult decisions, but the people have stuck with him because he knows them, and they know him. Just because the risk is serious, the problems significant, and the solutions urgent, DOC deliberately chooses how to use his bait approach to build rapport and belong so he can trust what needs to happen *will* happen.

The other approach modeled to him that he deliberately chooses *not* to emulate is a blaming and threatening approach from a senior leader named Dave. Dave used language and tone announcing threats like, "I will have your head on a pole if you don't do XYZ," with an audience of 150 people. As we explored in "Pause for Language," word choice, tone, and audience all have opportunities for others to experience us. It is an approach that some use but not the kind that aligns with DOC's brand and values. DOC talks about the amount of time this takes to really get to know people. Hitting on three of our key pillars—time, commitment, and belonging— his approach is a choice in how he spends his time and who he spends it with, building a connection and feeling and creating a sense of belonging so he's not lonely at the top.

At the top of the people function of a global consulting firm sits Nadia K. She is responsible for the policies that set expectation of decorum, models the example of all policies, establishes performance standards and adherence to them, and charges others to do the same. The double edge sword for Nadia's role is setting the bar high for performance and behavior while being relatable and accessible to establish trust. That is a fine line, and there is not a large margin of forgiveness if she finds herself too far on one side—either too rigid or too lenient. Yet she has toed this line for many years in different human and talent related positions. She describes her success to connect as being open to vulnerability. Sharing what is really going on in her world requires awareness of self and the commitment to share when the moment is offered. She shares the hardships of parenthood, a reality she lives raising three humans of her own with strong personalities, differing interests and activities, and schedules that tug at the time limits in a day. She brings people into decisions or process building while it is in formation to digest what may trigger the other person's emotions if it is something sensitive to their values or priorities, making them a part of instead of the recipients of a full baked outcome. She also opens herself up for the tough feedback she craves and fears in the same breath so that she can be more effective as a leader. Without the vulnerability and the clear experience she wants others to have of her, she misses the bait conversation opportunities getting side lined by a task or a facade of who she thinks people will see.

Dan Fisher combines his PhD in clinical psychology with his business acumen to transform leaders, teams, and organizations as a trusted advisor and executive coach. In Dan's early career, he coached individuals who were established as executives and very good at positioning themselves in the power dynamics of the organization. When he engaged with these very senior executives who had a lot of power and authority, he approached them not as the leader they are in the system they work, but rather as the human being who has a common experience with many other human beings—often in their role in their family. He finds this connection to be leveling in the relationship and to gain an awareness of where behaviors show up not just in the office, but often in our personal lives as well. This establishes a connection for him as an expert partner and also increases the awareness to the executive of how to create a connection to those in their organizational system.

In those early days of Dan's executive coaching days, he was working with a client who was very comfortable making other people uncomfortable. This leader was outcomes driven, and achieving the goal by any means necessary was his only path forward. His 360 feedback exposed how often he missed the opportunity to be supportive, to enable and empower others, and to connect on a human level. As coach and leader, Dan explored with him personality styles and how the needs and response of each of the styles are different. The style and approach he was missing was with those who are warm and accepting and value relationships. Dan went on to explain how collaborating and connecting with them would make the client a more powerful and influential leader—the antithesis of the impact he was having.

Unable to connect what he was hearing from his coach and his view of himself, he told Dan, "I hear you, but that's not me. And I'm very authentic, very genuine. I don't like to fake it. So, I don't think I can do that, because that is not me."

Not one to shy away from candor, Dan called out his client, doubting his assertion and challenging this self-limiting belief. He reframed the challenge as one of versatility—knowing what to do when, how, and how much. He assured the leader that he possessed the right tools in his personal toolbox to use in his work environment. He just needed know where to find them and when to deploy them. Dan then tapped into the family man, not the executive in the organization, and inquired about his daughters who were now in their early teens. Dan asked about when they were young and routines that involved human connection and collaboration—the art of reading stories and tucking them in to sleep. Dan had unlocked the human side of this challenging executive and was seeing a warm and sensitive dad who had just declared that is not authentic to who he is. While Dan was not suggesting he start reading bedtime stories to the people who worked for him, nor tuck them in, in the spirit of leadership versatility, he encouraged his client to engage that desire to be caring; to get to know people and let them know he is in their corner, he is rooting for them, and he is thinking about and committed to developing them. Dan highlighted the need to pull on some of the ways the client was successful at home and bring that to work and demonstrate connection.

People will follow leaders even when they make hard or unfavorable decisions when they know and trust the leader. Building this rapport, being seen as your true self even in your position, bolsters your followership when you intentionally share who you are, not just who you think you should show up to be.

Brené Brown defines connection as, "The energy that exists between people when they feel seen, heard, and valued; when they can give and receive without judgment and when they derive sustenance and strength form the relationship" (Brown 2022). To be seen, we must see ourselves first. We must also create the opportunities to be seen and see others— again, literally and figuratively. The pre-pandemic office cultures offered water cooler chats, stopping by offices to pop in and say hi, and hallway conversations to exchange ideas and personal nuggets of connection. We knew where we had a high probability of finding someone and engaging in an exchange while pouring coffee and getting a snack.

Along with many other things, the pandemic changed that convenience. For a few years we were all in, with kids, pets, non-work environments—all the filters abandoned in this frenzy of "new normal" that had nothing normal about it. Video calls were filled with the reminiscent Hollywood Squares style screen participants engaging in games and social activities to encourage everyone being seen, heard, and valued. The limiting beliefs or filters that traditionally held people back were suspended in the surrealness of ubiquitous experience of pandemic life.

That diminished in the novelty, and the rewards of connection were not as recognizable. The pause to take inventory of how others were experiencing each of us as leaders and how to convey that as a priority was quickly dismissed. Nothing replaced those virtual happy hours, costume and theme-based meetings, and coffee chats and office hours. Accessibility to leaders reverted to the closed-door meetings and diminished visibility of their *real* and non-work selves. The connections built during the pandemic quarantine abandoned even the most hierarchical of situations and removed the postures of positions on an org chart. Seniority didn't matter. People connected as people.

The nuance of hybrid work has yet to find a balance that strikes the impromptu opportunities and the intentional space to drive connection. The questions that once were so naturally "How are you, *really*?" have reverted to the bobber "pleasantries" to get to the agenda, the heart of the meeting, and the outcome drivers, avoiding the depth of curiosity about the person. These attempts to set boundaries are really just delusional barriers to meeting our needs of human connection and establishing rapport with those with commonalities to us. Pausing to ask the intentional questions drives engagement and connection with those you lead. Sharing your answers and engaging to be present drives *your* need to belong and connect.

Like with the blue house conversation, my need to belong and connect was void in the house we appropriately named "the Albatross." We made a financial decision to all live in the house and do work to prepare to sell it for our next step, but in hindsight it was a Blended Family 101 mistake. Jeff and I indexed on the financial prioritization and stabilization of three of our four kids. We completely neglected engaging in the conversation about what would be best for us and then how to meet the needs of all six of us as we began our marital union. At the time, the bobber conversation felt safer than diving into the abyss to go after the bait.

How are you prepared for bait discussions and recognize when you are giving in to the ease of showing up as a bobber, skimming the surface and resisting the connection?

PAUSE FOR PRACTICE
- ▶ There are many levels of listening: background noise, listening or interrupting to get your point in, deep and active listening to be fully present and curious.
  - ◆ When was the last time someone really listened to you?
  - ◆ How did you know? What were the indicators?
  - ◆ How did you feel when you felt heard?

- Capture this awareness and how you describe the person who was truly listening to you. What made that experience a bait versus bobber conversation?

▶ Equally important, when was the last time you really listened to someone else—gave them your undivided, unpolluted attention? Target committing to this at least once a week—being fully present and focused on what the person is saying with their words, their body language, their tone, their cadence, and their other cues.

▶ Reflect on your week and identify a bobber interaction you had. What might the outcome have been had you gone deeper—bait like?

  - What got in your way of having a bait conversation?
  - What impression did you create, and does it align with what you want others to experience?

▶ Think about what is coming up—meetings, dinner with old friends, a phone call with a family member, an in-office day, parenting time with your stepkids—and identify where you typically default to moving quickly, maybe even labeling the interaction as pleasantries.

  - How will you show up differently?
  - What is one thing you will commit to do intentionally that will align to how you want others to feel from a connection point with you?

PAUSE FOR PRACTICE PAGE

Pause for Laughter

"A sense of humor is part of the art of leadership, of getting along with people, of getting things done."

—DWIGHT D. EISENHOWER

PRESIDENT OF THE UNITED STATES (1953–1961)

For Corey's fourteenth birthday, her first since I was a part of her life, we went to dinner at a big chain restaurant. We had the combined gang out to celebrate her, and it felt exhilarating. Each of the kids ordered a sugar explosion carbonated drink, most of them loaded with grenadine for the added burst. The restaurant was Corey's choice, and she knew what she wanted to order, but we were all enjoying the time to sit at a big round table together and savor the moment. Until… the tray of their sodas, Roy Rogers, and Shirley Temples, rich with soda syrup and grenadine, had arrived and the server lost the balance of the tray. Those very cold, sticky, ice filled libations dumped right down my back. My eyes grew wide as I looked straight across the table at Corey, who was in shock as if she could feel the chill down my spine. I calmly stood and walked to the restroom, ice cubes falling off my back with each step.

Corey met me in the bathroom, where we let out the laughter we had held in so as to not embarrass the server.

A couple of weeks later, I took three of our four kids to a local pizza parlor. At the drink counter, we placed an order for a pitcher of root beer. The iconic nugget ice that packed the salad bar, insulating the toppings piled high in metal containers, also crowded the plastic pitcher with the icy root beer filling the gaps and flowing to the brim. The young teen working behind the counter filling this drink order was quite taken by Corey's beauty and had a difficult time taking his eyes off her—so much so that when he went to put the pitcher packed with the soda and ice on the counter, he overstretched and missed the edge, dumping the pitcher over the top of young Ellie. It was cold, sticky, and wet, and I knew exactly how Ellie felt physically. But I had years of age on her mere five as she stood with the root beer saturating her Peter Pan collared white shirt and coordinating outfit. She was very embarrassed and cold in spite of being truly a victim of an unfortunate circumstance.

I knew if I looked up at Corey and we locked eyes, the laughter would be out of control. I also knew that me laughing was not what my daughter needed from her mom. Corey was not about to do anything, even as an early teen, that compromised the feeling of that five-year-old Ellie. We went to the bathroom to get Ellie dried off, did a carousel of clothes trading to get her into something dry, and returned to enjoy dinner. Ellie was and still is the most resilient human I have ever known.

The first restaurant situation where I received the tray of drinks, I went into the evening knowing how special I wanted Corey to feel on her birthday. This dinner was to celebrate *her*, and I spent time thinking about how she would feel. The location, the gifts, the time—each detail mattered. When the drinks dumped on me, my expectation and clarity for the night was beneficial, as I did not spring up shouting (though it was a shock and warranted that) but instead stayed calm in my seat and looked straight across at her trying to hold back her laughter. I offered Corey the permission to laugh and for me to know it was not *at* me but because we were sharing the situation. I did not make a scene, nor did I request we leave so I could get out of the sticky, wet mess. This was not about me, and I would ensure it remained that way.

The pizza parlor debacle was a bit more challenging. It was just a night with three of the kids, and those times were easy back then. They enjoyed being with me and I with them. It was some pizza at a local haunt, and I didn't need to prepare for what might get in the way. But when that pitcher of icy cold soda poured like a fountain over young Ellie, I had that moment of power. The liquid flowing was the stimulus. My reaction had yet to surface, so I held onto that pause to collect my breath and decide. As a mom, in my core I knew it was my job to keep my girl safe—even from emotions and humility—so delayed laughter at the situation prevailed. Resilient Ellie came around quickly once we had the wardrobe change, and we all laughed heartily. We *still* laugh heartily about that memory. It's a bond, and laughter will do that.

Laughter can also alienate and be cruel. The senior leader who prides themself on being in on all the "inside jokes" but fails to make connections with those they lead fails to see the alienation of the laughter. They are the one who is sitting at a huge meeting with no one around. They find amusement by something one of their peers on the main stage said, but have no one to share it with. They are the ones who show up taking themselves too seriously and missing the opportunity to relax into the moment and the opening it offers to build rapport and connection.

Susan, our fearless chief human resources officer from "Pause for Clarity," brought the gumption of laughing wounds to that board room in NYC. In her pre-teen heartthrob years, she held closely her secret of the crush she carried on the cute boy in her class. She found the courage to share this secret with her best friend, trusting the confidence of the friendship and female bonds. Tragically, for a twelve-year-old child, her friend, unable to contain the growing secret inside her, exploded like a balloon in the hot sun. Susan's closely held secret crush was now the central focus of the crowd of friends amassed on the playground together at recess. With blood rushing to her innocent face, Susan stood in horror as all the kids laughed—the common and inappropriate response when emotions or news is shared—and others were left not knowing what to do with it. What might have been a form of nervous laughter form her peers was jeering to her ears.

The deep wounds of the feeling of being laughed *at* traversed years of academic success, new jobs, career highs and lows, accomplishments, and devoted love from her forever crush and husband. What others forgot about and likely don't remember on that sunny afternoon among the swings and jungle gym, Susan had translated it into a behavior pattern of holding back her feelings, closing off others and resisting vulnerability. As she matured, she reflected on the impact and made the choice to shut down the narrative of doubting her self-worth and instead grew into her confidence. That shift is what propelled the strong CHRO to take a stand and demonstrate her strength and clarity of her value.

The complicated facets of laughter warrant many ongoing studies. Looking at laughter in the workplace, the needle points to it having a positive impact on team performance, collaboration, trust, resilience, and leadership behaviors. A growing body of work is also underfoot to look more systematically at the consistency of studying humor and the differentiation of having a sense of humor versus demonstrating a humorous experience. Indications show there is a correlation of humor to followership and that its effects vary by situation (Kong et al. 2019; Rosenberg et al. 2021). Levity, lightness, and permission to have fun fall in the column of having a sense of humor. Even the most buttoned up and serious people have a need to connect, which we will touch more on in "Pause for Belonging." Humor and laughter and delivering quality work are not mutually exclusive.

When people laugh it is an indication they are present, because it is an in the moment response to a stimulus. When more than one person is laughing together, they are having a shared experience in the moment. That presence is aligned to the here and now. Knowing your values, knowing how you want others to experience you, and being clear on the impact you want to create frees you from laughing when it is not appropriate (making fun of someone or a situation that compromises another) and allows you to quickly laugh when the moment is amusing and appropriate. In the snap moment of power, you more quickly recognize where the humor falls on that axis.

When was the last time you laughed so hard you cried? I was shocked to hear from some of my closest friends that they have never had this experience. I thought this was something *everyone* had experienced. But they haven't, and I now have a new understanding of levels of laughter and how the spectrum is not the same for everyone. For some leaders, tapping into humor can be uncomfortable. It requires a vulnerability to connect with others, similar to making small talk. Having a sense of humor versus finding humor in different things opens the honest expression of how you engage with the world and where you find joy. Some leaders struggle to share their hobbies with others in fear of being judged. Humor can be similar. Yet, what if you share that and find a deeper connection? Or are present and clear enough about your lightheartedness to be able to laugh when the moment presents itself?

No one, and I mean *no one*, has more fun together than my three stepkids. Even in their early to mid-thirties, they can laugh more than an audience at the best comedy club. This has been a trademark from the early days of knowing them. The first time I formally met them, Jeff took me into their house to introduce me. They lined up along the wall to say hello and hit me with questions referring to my inventory of jokes and peppering me with theirs. The final query was from ten-year-old Scott asking if I could wiggle my ears. (The answer is no but I am still practicing.) You guessed it, he can, and they all laughed and have been laughing together ever since. They can bring each other to tears through any situation—painful surgeries, tragedy, unfortunate circumstances, happy times and the whole spectrum. It is passion filled and fun to watch. But it can quickly leave out others around them.

When others are laughing and you are not clued in, it can generate fear you are the butt of the laughter. Like anything, laughter has a dark side, but typically it is rewarding. The saying, "We are laughing *with* you, not *at* you, so hurry up and laugh," doesn't often bring out the warm fuzzy feelings being included on the joke induces. Yet our brains respond positively to things that provide emotional connection, and laughter proves to be a driver of inclusion—and a great form of therapy (Barker 2017). Ensuring you are not laughing alone or laughing with a group minus one or two is an opportunity to connect and encourage others to feel a sense of belonging. When you are the one not laughing, don't shy away from inquiring to be included in the joy—or stating your reality of what is not funny.

Pre-pandemic I traveled to one of our offices in another city. I borrowed someone's office who was out for the day to work from and take calls. This person was very particular. Everything had its place, and the precision made it clear this was important to them. Another colleague realized whose office I was in and suggested I move just one thing—a book, the stapler, anything. We had a little chuckle when we talked about it, but I did not move a thing. While that seemed funny, I have a core value of respect. Being in someone else's space, with their things and their set-up, and moving it to disrupt what I observed as a clear value of order or discipline to them did not seem funny. At another point in time, I shared with the office owner the temptation and my refrain. I was greeted with mild appreciation, but louder was a stern warning of how funny that would *not* have been to them. If we don't pause to recognize the harm our humor may cause, we can miss out on the clues core to someone's values and overstep.

Levity and psychological safety are elements of demonstrating a sense of humor. One of my clients works in a high intensity and fast paced environment. The work they do is impacting a better world and renewable energy—not something to be taken lightly. They hold the work they do, the timelines they do it, and each other to a high standard. While the work is serious, my client reflected that seriousness through his facial expressions, or lack thereof, and engagement with others. As is often the challenge, he was having difficulty getting people to see how hard his team was working and demonstrating an appreciation for their efforts while holding them accountable to results. Feedback indicated his smile was very disarming, and people felt more relaxed when they saw him smile. He started smiling more and naming his expressions since what people observed typically did not match what he was feeling. For example, with a straight face he would say, "This is my excited face." Cracking a smile quickly upon finishing the statement offers a self-teasing insight to his humanity and offered the opportunity to connect.

Others observe us, not knowing if we know how we come across. When we indicate to others we do and are lighthearted about it, we are all in on the inside joke, or at least we all now have the same knowledge. The impact my client is experiencing is people are more open with him, are sharing more information, and are more collaborative, and he is enjoying that shift. The benefit others are experiencing is having some fun while still working hard to imminent deadlines of big and meaningful work.

The myth is that lack of humor is somehow correlated with capability, or a stiff image indicates higher quality. If you are offering opportunities for some humor, it diminishes your impact or sets a tone for others that is normalizing mediocrity. Humor can be how we drive awareness or find a way to relate to a situation or emotion. Funny Business is a card deck of cartoons depicting situations of work-related topics widely used by coaches and HR professionals to deepen conversations, uncover truths, and address conflicts. Creator Paul Damiano refers to the approach as not *ha-ha* humor but *a-ha* awareness, which is followed by a chuckle. The ability to see ourselves in situations that are relatable makes us human—even vulnerable. When we share vulnerabilities away from defensiveness, we open ourselves to connection.

As mentioned, sharing a few laughs creates connection. But how do you learn how to create the lightness? Improv training for professionals and laughter workshops are a thing—for real! Organizations invest a lot of money to "train" and *experience* humor and the environment it creates to enjoy its stress reducing value. Fear based cultures are evident in the lack of smiles in the halls and break rooms. Fear of market, fear of punishment, fear of rejection—it can signal all sorts of fear or lack of engagement. Smiles are contagious, so it takes very little to start to impact that culture. The endorphin release initiates the feel-good chemicals and prompts others to follow your expression even unwillingly.

While I was working at the Center for Creative Leadership, successful organizations and individuals were coming for solutions to improve their capabilities and the business outcomes through their people. They invested a lot of resources—time and money, at the top of the list. We had serious work to do and needed to be innovative in our solutions and create an environment for people to relax into their authentic selves. Our team of colleagues lived this in the psychological safety that was demonstrated by leadership and how we engaged with each other. Laughter was free in the hallways, and solutions were well defined and articulated. We did not sacrifice one for the other while we flowed between the two, never straying from the path of excellence. It didn't hurt that my closest colleague was also part of an improv group outside of work. There was no such thing as mundane while we worked together. He made everything fun, and I was a willing audience laugh track.

The contagious nature of smiling and laughter is generally a good thing but is risky when it is inappropriate. Do you notice who isn't laughing when you are with a group? Address if they feel left out, if your humor is offensive or just not funny, or if there is something else. It's possible they didn't hear what was said, but getting clarity on this can shift the feeling of belonging and your understanding of how your humor is impacting others and who shares a sense of humor with you.

Remember, be prepared. Do the work ahead of time to take inventory of what is funny, what is not, and what might seem funny but might leave a different impression depending on the audience. Think about where you might be showing up too strict or someplace you can offer a smile more freely. This preparation reflects your decision to be intentional in the moment, to be present, and be aware and notice.

PAUSE FOR PRACTICE

- ► What makes you laugh or even chuckle?
  - ♦ Do you know the last time you laughed?
  - ♦ What prompted it?
- ► When was the last time you made someone else laugh?
  - ♦ What did you do or say? What was the situation and the surrounding?
  - ♦ Were you being intentional, or did it naturally happen?
  - ♦ Who wasn't laughing? Did you notice?
  - ♦ When you see others not laughing, what is a way to check in with them to be able to see their values?
- ► What is something you might laugh at that, when reflecting, might not have been aligned to what you want others to see of you? It might be a joke that pokes at a compromised population, or a group with an identity you support but your joining in undermined that allyship. Maybe you didn't laugh but you also didn't stop others to draw awareness to what is not funny about the situation.
  - ♦ How will you be more intentional with your laughter and outward expression to align to your values and intent?

PAUSE FOR PRACTICE PAGE

Pause for Belonging

"Loneliness does not come from having no people around you, but from being unable to communicate the things that seem important to oneself."

—CARL JUNG

SWISS PSYCHOLOGIST AND PSYCHOANALYST

FOUNDER OF ANALYTICAL PSYCHOLOGY

"Megan says you all blame everything on her." The therapist tossed the statement as he leaned back in his chair, pen poised to capture the fallout from his opening line. It backfired on him when my oldest stepdaughter, Robyn, replied with, "We do!" The lack of defensiveness and the full admission of the truth warranted his startled reaction, and what followed was not the blended family therapy we were planning to help us engage in a more aligned way.

Robyn went on to describe that they (the three kids my husband brought to our marriage who were fifteen, thirteen, and ten when we met) knew logically I had nothing to do with most of the things they were grappling with, but I was the easy target. Other therapists had described the challenge I faced in my new role as the one who was not in a position of trust. Mom and Dad naturally hold a position of trust to their kids. Mom was now in a loving relationship with the family and community favorite and beloved fourth grade teacher, putting her in a position of trust, and I was new to each and all of them. Regardless of reality, I was a stranger.

My drive to succeed in this role was high, but my capability and experience was not matched for the position. My parents are still happily married, I did not have a model of a blended family that was healthy, and the ones Disney portrayed were not inclusive of the stepmom I envisioned being. My peers were just starting to have kids and were not resources for teen years, and as a mother of a five-year-old, I had yet to experience any of this from an adult perspective.

My approach to engage the best resources and upskill was through routes of therapists who see this more often than I had. Jeff and I met with individual therapists, then found the "best" to work with our blended family. Our initial meeting with the selected provider included us sharing how much emotion there is and how bringing all three kids at the same time seemed like a lot. We trusted his expertise when he told us that was the best approach and that he would manage it. His opening line was a mic drop, not a conversation starter. As the truth unfolded of how the kids saw me and my role, he sat stunned, as if he was enjoying popcorn and Coke while watching a full feature movie. We stuck with the therapy for a few sessions, but when the kids pointed out we went in talking and all getting along to not speaking to each other when we left, then maybe the sessions were not serving our purpose.

Blended family therapy had failed to deliver on the resource and support I needed it to be. It felt pretty lonely, and I did not feel like I was at the top.

The mantra that it is lonely at the top is widespread while climbing the ranks to higher level positions within companies. If there is a CEO stepmom of a blended family, the other stepmom in our family held that position. She was in the enviable state to have already built the relationships and establishing her positional power seat before being visibly in the role of their mom's girlfriend. The advantage was going from having very clear boundaries about teacher-student roles and progressing out of those roles to let the more personal connections develop, which is far easier than the reverse order of being friendly and personal then needing more distance for hierarchy.

Ascending from peer to boss with the same audience presents that set of challenges when you are friendly with those on your team you are now charged to be "boss" over. Connecting with people at work is important, and having those meaningful relationships are core to our being. We learn this through Maslow's hierarchy of needs, which establishes that as each level of needs are sufficiently met, we can move up to meet the next level needs. An illustration of this hierarchy is represented below. The most basic level is that of food, water, and shelter, then we can address our need to be safe and secure in our health and employment and that of our friends and families. The next level in the hierarchy is love and belonging—friendship, family, and a sense of connection. Building on this is where we experience confidence and self-esteem, then ultimately self-actualization—our ultimate purpose (Maslow 1943). We spend most of our time at work, so having meaningful connections increases our efficacy and engagement and moves us toward greater purpose. Yet the higher people go, if they are not intentional about maintaining and building those connections, inevitably they begin to isolate themselves.

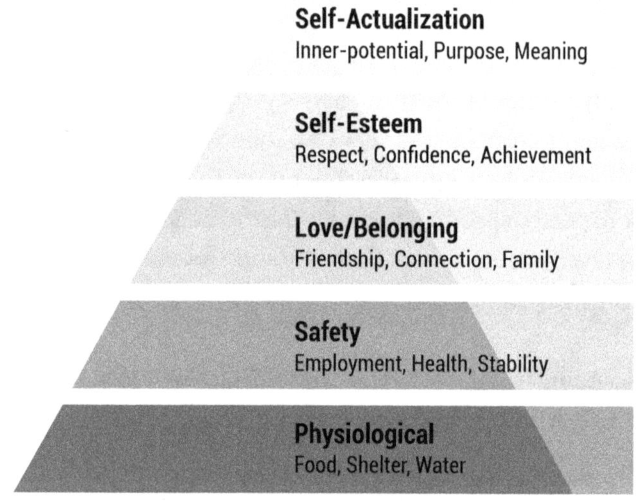

Maslow's Hierarchy of Needs

The stories we tell ourselves about the need to isolate the more senior you climb on the proverbial ladder center around perception and boundaries. Senior leaders tell me they don't want to be viewed as complaining, or they don't want to show up not taking the high road and have concerns around being friends versus "boss." There is an opportunity to be *both* friend *and* boss. How you define those boundaries and hold yourself and others accountable to the job and performance expectations with consistent professional treatment of all is what allows space to foster those connections. The perception of what others will see and judge becomes the barrier to intentional choice of seeing *how* you as the leader want to feel connection. Pausing to consider how you establish belonging and fitting in allows you to then navigate the freedom within the boundaries you implement. This can allow you to check the assumptions you might have made that you cannot have connections with people who report to you and instead allow yourself the flexibility to notice where you are drawn to connect and feel a sense of belonging.

Those boundaries might look like sharing enough to be relatable and establishing a connection without gushing details. When you are going through challenges, share you are having a hard time without the gory details of what is making it hard and who is involved. Think back to your brand and your values. Knowing what you stand for and how you want to be known will guide the level of detail you share and create awareness of what challenges you might create by not sticking to these principles. The balance is what it will take for you to feel the sense of connection and seeing yourself *in* the organization against creating the space for others to feel connected and belong on the other side of the scale. It is weighing *your* needs against your servant leadership style.

Where lines get blurred is when the friendship between a boss and direct reports is evidenced in the comings and goings of the office, when it creates a feeling of others being left out. This also shows up in "Pause for Laughter" when others are obviously omitted from an "inside joke." Holding clear edges around the visibility of the connection and friendship reduces other's concern of equitable and fair performance expectations and accountability. Pausing to consider the implications with the void of Maslow's third level of needs stands to compromise your ability to build and grow self-respect and esteem. Sourcing those connections within your company is not the only way to accomplish meeting this level of love and belonging. Other ways to combat the loneliness and isolation is to bring along your relationships from other organizations and to rely on your peer group. This peer group may be internal to your organization, in your industry, or more broadly from your level in any industry and can stem from many pathways.

Noah Rabinowitz is a learning and development leader with a LinkedIn following of more than 27,000 people. Noah created a seven-part LinkedIn series he calls ALP (adversity/learning/purpose). In these seven posts he shares his challenges, his vulnerabilities, and his hope. He opened dialogue to navigating illness, loss, and self-doubt as some of the frequently named topics of isolation as you climb in leader levels—those topics you cannot share with others and have open conversations about. His posts drove engagement and dialogue and opened others up to their challenges. His role at the time was in a large corporation in a very senior and visible position. His take away at the conclusion of the series was his need for empathy, and in order to receive empathy, he has to share and to show up to hear others and be in the space with them. This is a new angle on servant leadership—one that centers on intentionality and clarity of self and brand with openness and inviting others to come *to* you, the leader.

Let's revisit servant leadership from "Pause to Show Up." Greenleaf's essay rooted servant leadership in the core principles of listening, persuasion, access to intuition and foresight, use of language, and pragmatic measurements of outcomes (Greenleaf 1970). In the evolution since his original writing of 1970, the core tenants fundamentally rely on leaders abandoning their needs in order to serve others; for leaders to know where their people are and meet them there without an inventory of their own needs.

In a deeply personal dialogue during an episode of *We Can Do Hard Things*, Glennon Doyle and Kelly Clarkson discuss the art of ending marriages. The podcast conversation has some rich threads about losing self in marriage, which we also see as leaders become more. Most notably is Glennon sharing how giving to others and not receiving, the core of servant leadership, leaves emptiness with nothing left to give (Doyle 2023). This is where servant leaders hit burnout. And that is not serving anyone well.

Meg Greenhouse accepted a senior vice president position of a European e-commerce company in Germany, moving from her native home in the United States before ever seeing the country she was about to call home. Not long after taking her leadership post, the company holiday party came. There was a lot of buzz and excitement—her first signal this was a bit different from corporate holiday gatherings in the US. Party day arrived, and Meg was looking forward to experiencing the culture that accompanied the festivities of her new environment. She was greeted to the party with free flowing beverages, counter to the more litigious hazards in the US where many a career ends, not advances, at holiday parties. Meg recognized how others engaged and the importance of what the party offered them, but she did not see herself in that engagement. What she realized is that being a part of the antics did not fit her needs, but finding *her* way to belong was important. You can now find Meg tending the bar in the early hours of the shindig. She is able to honor her boundaries and rapport while serving her entire team their drinks, singing and dancing with them and leaving early without sharing libations with them. Meg's team deserves a leader they can look up to, she believes, and she has clarity of who she wants them to see when they look up to her. She follows that with meeting their needs, so in her servant leadership style, she shows up and pours their drinks, sings and dances with them for a bit, and makes an early exit.

At the same time, Meg explores where she can let her hair down, as that is the barrier she sees that creates loneliness at the top. When you know more of the inner workings of the company and what is around the bend, there is knowledge you cannot share more broadly. Meg's approach is to find one or two people she connects with and establish that camaraderie. She then keeps those friendships discreet, so much so that it was not until long after she left one company that others realized how close she was with one of their colleagues. But that friendship kept her from feeling isolated and lonely, and she was able to see herself belonging and creating space for others to feel their belonging too.

Boundaries are a key element to managing the knowledge leaders have access to and connecting with people within the organization—even those outside the organization—and recognizing what can and can't be shared. Those boundaries establish protection from wrongdoing and also insulate the relationships established within those boundaries.

Elton, our star collegiate athlete and D&I practitioner, is also a dad and stepdad. As a single dad, he brought his son to the union joining with his wife's two children. They added a fourth together to complete their family. He relates the challenge of boundaries as the organizational leader with the one in blended families too. The raw emotion of wanting to wrap up all the kids, to pull them in and put up the walls and insulate "our" family, is so real. Also real is how the shared kids have other parents and another family they are also members of. This highlights the complexity of boundaries for inclusion, not exclusion; using language and speaking the names of the other parents to create a safe space to openly talk about them without conflict. Allowing the kids to talk about the other parent without judgment, letting them share what is on their heart, and leaning into that as a connection with the kids is an important lens to focus.

Setting boundaries (knowing what and how much to share), being relatable, time for self-care, the balance of giving and receiving, and experiencing human connection but not isolating and withdrawing is the equivalent of the flight instructions in the case of loss of cabin pressure: Put your oxygen mask on before you help others.

PAUSE FOR PRACTICE

▶ Isolating yourself from others who are mostly positive in your world and to you isn't usually intentional. This can be a slow and subtle process, and the connection slowly fades. Pause and notice who you are not connecting with.

♦ Who has been a supporter, a friend, a colleague, a customer, a boss—someone whom you shared a personal connection and you have lost or lessened that relationship?

♦ Identify why that has happened and explore the value in reigniting that or where you will get what that served elsewhere.

▶ Often it is easier to see when others are losing touch or promoting into an isolated space.

♦ Who do you notice is not connecting in the workplace?

♦ Who is going through a hard time—maybe even a divorce, maybe working to blend a family—and not connecting with others?

♦ How can you reach out to them to offer a connection?

▶ Another great misnomer is tricking ourselves into believing we can be two different people—one at home and one at work. We are still one person, so that misconception instead leaves others confused about who you are.

♦ Create a Möbius strip (or cut out the outline on the following page).

■ Cut the edge of a plain piece of paper (about eight inches long and 1.5 inches wide).

■ Label each of the corners with A and C on one end and B and D on the other end.

■ On the side with the letters, list all the things about you that are your "at home" self—the things you don't want to or just don't naturally share at work; your inside world. On the other side, list all the things about you that are your "professional" self, a.k.a. your outside world.

- Now twist the A-C side a half-turn and bring it to the B-D side. Match the A corner to the D corner, and B to C, and tape the edges together to create a flow and connection.
- It should look like this:

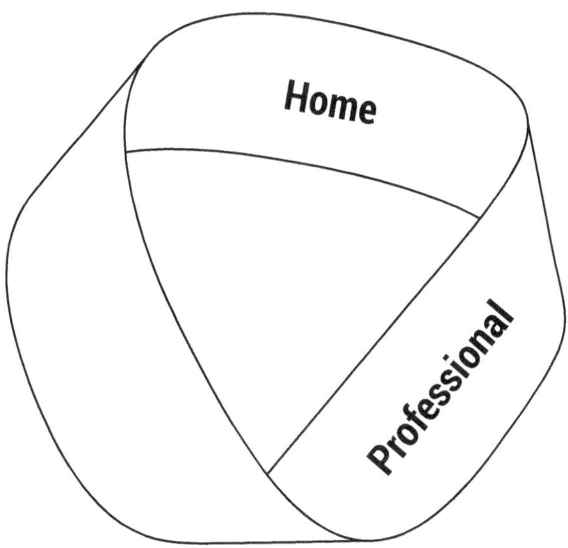

► What do you notice about the flow and connection of your inside and outside worlds? Where are your values and brand most obvious? Where are they clouded and could be clearer?

PAUSE FOR PRACTICE PAGE

PAUSE FOR PRACTICE PAGE

A   C

B   D

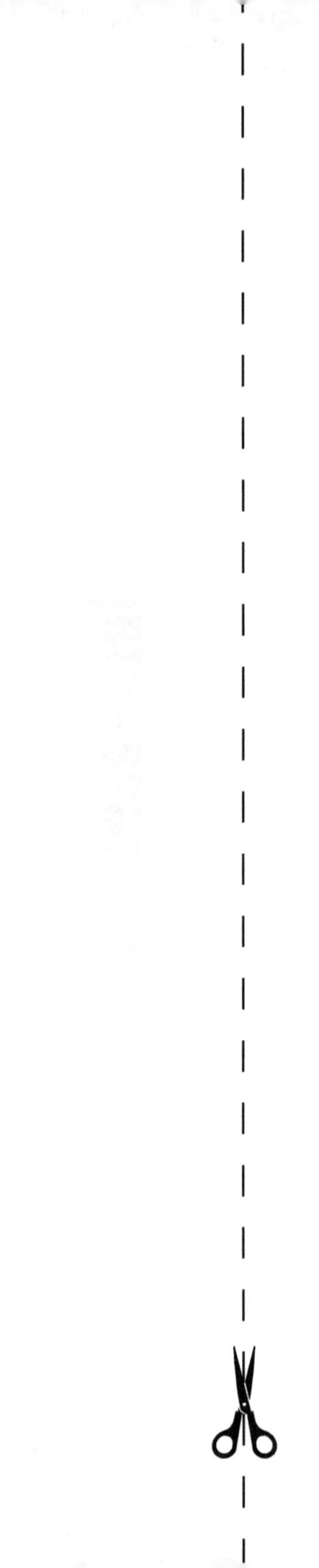

Pause for Your Journey

"If you want to be a grocer, or a general, or a politician, or a judge, you will invariably become it; that is your punishment. If you never know what you want to be, if you live what some might call the dynamic life but what I will call the artistic life, if each day you are unsure of who you are and what you know you will never become anything, and that is your reward."

—OSCAR WILDE, AUTHOR

"WHERE DO YOU SEE YOURSELF IN FIVE YEARS?"

I heard a thud when the interviewing panel asked the question, as if it had landed on the tile floor I was pacing while holding my flip phone to my ear.

A five-year plan? I was barely thirty, on the other side of a divorce, and a single mom to a toddler. The only thing I could definitively say was how getting divorced and being a single mom had never been part of any plan I might have conjured up. Anything beyond my current status was subject to the tenuous balance of career and single motherhood.

"If I had a plan for five years, I would have missed out on so many great opportunities that have brought me to where I am now," I said to the void of interviewers in the abyss on the other end.

That answer was raw and honest, and it omitted any insight to what I had in mind for the next five years, which was survival—literally! My response sparked a different conversation than the panel expected. Rather than the well thought-out articulated response of my plan to navigate from a strategically mapped position with skills to master before moving to the next scripted stop on my professional journey, I was describing a route of growth and self-awareness. Certainly, an award-winning sales rep, such as myself, interviewing for a position at her alma mater had a master plan that this opportunity fit nicely into. But I did not have a master plan. What I did have were clear values that served as my compass to point me in the direction of what was next.

My career aspirations varied from veterinarian to teacher to astronaut, but the only thing I knew for certain from an early age was I wanted to be a mom. As I navigated my divorce and single parenting, I was still certain of this and grateful for my daughter. I was not yet thirty when my divorce became final, and my dreams of many kids became a reality of one amazing daughter. Equally as clear was what I did *not* want to be. I did *not* want to be a stepmother. I knew my strengths as a mom and was not sure those would translate well as a stepmom. The references of my friend's "stepmonsters" dimmed the consideration, much like the lack of interest I had in many of my early childhood career aspirations once I learned what the positions actually entailed.

Just like that lack of master career plan, I also did not spend my early years dreaming about "when I grow up and my marriage falls apart and I get divorced and am a single mom I will…" This also limited my ability to envision what being a stepmom *could* look like, what it *could* feel like, how I *could* show up aligned to those big values and aspirations of connectedness, and how stepparenting could be another outlet to demonstrate the opportunity for unchartered paths. Those limitations I fenced myself in went so far as me creating a short list of dating "rules," and one was not dating anyone who had kids. Then I met Jeff, who then introduced me to his kids. My journey shifted in a direction I had not anticipated, and it was uniquely mine.

Just like relationships, not all career paths are linear. Not all companies have mapped career paths for employees to follow. The military and civil servants, like fire departments, have paths, ranks, time, and test requirements that provide a clear road map. Some companies have similar structures to growing in roles and experience to earn promotions and new job titles. It can be very clear and almost curriculum like. Yet some companies embrace you being the designer of your career during your tenure under their brand. You just can't always count on the organization to provide this path and clarity for you.

You met Emily two years into her career in "Pause for Clarity" when she was navigating conflict with a peer and learning different approaches to diffuse those situations. She continued her journey at Procter & Gamble to a position leading a team of designers. When she was promoted into the role, she inherited the team from her predecessor. She did not recruit and hire them but instead stepped in as their boss. An ambitious member of her new direct reports had a career plan, and the next waypost was in her sights. She possessed a strong work ethic and brand for getting things done and driving change—especially as it related to inclusion. This team member was laser focused on a director level promotion and saw her new relatable ambitious boss as her ally in this aim. Inspired by the strengths this woman demonstrated, Emily wanted to be a part of her success story.

Emily saw her impact and confidently told her she absolutely deserved to be promoted, but Emily told her that *she* would never promote her. The caveat was that Emily saw this woman deserved a director level position, but she did not have an opening available on her team, as she only had designers. More significant was the fact this woman was not a designer, and being promoted to a director-level position on a team not in her area of expertise would hinder her success and future growth. What Emily *did* do was to tell her to find the openings in the organization at that level where she had relationships, and Emily would serve as her ally.

At first blush, her decision sounds like a shutdown. But the message around the decision is: "I promote you into a designer position. You're not a designer, and now I've just stalled your career instead of accelerating it. You deserve to accelerate. Let me help you with acceleration. You didn't hear no, you heard yes, not here." The approach of recognizing and guiding *where* to be promoted ensured success on the career path her new team member had designed for herself. The shift just took a more definitive and likely squarer right turn than the promotion first appeared. The variables of the path should be considered: Is it the right promotion to succeed? Or will the promotion put you in a place of failure or stall your career? These are significant differences warranting a pause for clarity.

Knowing when a career plan serves you versus holding you back is a key differentiator. Having goals that involve steps and criteria cannot be manufactured. For example, becoming a medical practitioner requires specific course work, degrees, graduate level tests, and applications to medical school or PA or nurse practitioner programs accompanied by hours of shadowing in the field. A plan must be in place to launch this journey. Those jobs and careers that are not anchored in technical expertise, testing, and or benchmarks offer more opportunity for creativity. Those paths include exploration, noticing what might be different and exciting or discovering new areas that awaken energy to seize the moment—which only *you* can determine.

Sometimes you have a career path and destination, but it shifts. For example, a young mother of two was recently promoted to a senior vice president role in a Fortune 100 company. She is settling into her position, leaning into leading at a higher level and being more strategic. She is clear in her challenges, her new growth edge, and is receiving positive feedback that she is succeeding—more specifically that she is exceeding expectations. The position was her *big* career goal; the end game. Now that she has made it to this space, she wonders, *Is this it? Am I missing something, or is there more?* She had a path. She knew what she wanted. And once there, she realized she could and wanted to do more. Her plan is now shifting. It is growing with her.

When thinking about plans, how far out can you map? Does your path allow for growth and the unexpected opportunities along the way? The board game Life made entertainment out of college, jobs and marital and parenting status. When she was merely eight years old, Carolyn Buck Luce started living her own game of life and designed The Decade Game. In her book, Buck Luce references these types of goals as ten-year destinations. She has guided others to think differently: designing your own best decade and not playing someone else's game. She reminds us to stop trying to do what you think others expect of you or what you are supposed to do and design your own journey to get to your ten year destination. In Carolyn's game guide, destinations are based on pillars that represent values, not titles or positions. The pillars to build your vision are based on your stand which is your values. The five pillars are self, others, craft, contributions, and learning. The model encourages self-growth in areas that feed one's soul and encourages growth in community, professionalism, and the whole self of contentment. Carolyn encourages her readers to dream big goals, big enough they take every last bit of ten years to accomplish, resulting in the whole person development, not a one dimensional professional. This approach is a move away from career pathing and goal setting for positions as milestones. However, The Decade Game also recognizes we all need milestones and achievement along the way. By recognizing and mapping "tiny mighties," we can identify those small steps of accomplishments currently within your reach on your way to your ten-year destination (Luce 2022).

The approach of The Decade Game® connects to develop more holistically, which leans on clarity of what you want out of life and how you want to impact others or your business. It is easy to get mired in what is happening around us or the narrative within organizations.

When I was a consultant in a large firm, I was staffed on clients who hired us to come in and fix problems—cash flow, profit margins, creating new processes, navigating change and bringing others along, and so on. My work with clients was challenging, but it was getting further away from the type of coaching and leadership development that was my sweet spot. Every client I worked on was a client of a partner in my firm. They had sourced the client, sold the work, and defined the work streams and what we would be held accountable to deliver. As I became restless, defining recruiting and onboarding strategies and executing them, creating talent retention plans and implementing best in class communication strategies, and leading change initiatives, I was tapped to use my talents in a different area of the firm. Our conversations progressed to define a new space for us both that would benefit the firm. This presented a new challenge and opportunity, but it also left a conversation to be had with the partner who owned this client relationship to discuss how to roll me off the client work to go to the new team and focus on developing our internal resources instead of clients.

In this highly matrixed organization, the move would require my soon to be "boss" to negotiate with my current "boss." This call happened, and we were set to progress. That was good. I felt relief this would be smooth and actually happen. But my phone rang the next day, and it was my current "boss." He heard I wanted to move to an internal team and focus on building the coaching program for the firm. Rather than releasing me from the project and working behind the scenes, he called to hear what I wanted, because he wanted to hear it from me. His inquiry was one supporting my career aspirations and path, though confusing to most in a consulting firm because I was choosing to leave the revenue generation side of the firm to the back-office function. This narrative that you always want to be as close to the revenue stream as possible so you are not at risk when the market turns is a loud soundtrack in any organization like this one. My pause to be clear in what was important to me to grow was challenged with the support from this leader. His concern and care about my intent—ensuring he heard it from me and not taking someone else's word for it—felt validating. Kindly, he left the door open for me to come back to "the dark side" (what he referred to the client facing, revenue generating side of the business) when I was ready. The impact of his call and support showed me that my choice meant I was charting my own career path. And more importantly, I knew I had leadership support.

Sometimes opportunities surface outside of your current organization and appear even when you are happy in what you are doing. An early career professional was happy in her position when a position with a broader berth of responsibility than what she was doing caught her eye. She threw her hat in the ring and was offered the job. She accepted the offer (after some impressive negotiations). She was leaving a job where she grew and gained great experience, which greatly contributed to her presenting as an outstanding candidate for the position she had just secured. Not wanting to let anyone down or to be seen as unappreciative of the opportunities afforded her, she was nervous about giving her notice. She paused, thought about what was driving her to go after the new opportunity, how that aligned to how she wanted to be experienced, and how she wanted others to experience her in the company she was leaving. Once she was clear on that, she engaged in her departure dialogue. The conversations that surrounded her exit were wrapped in sincerity and encouragement to go and learn and be successful. They also included an invitation to return.

The point is that paths are not always linear, nor are they always clear. Getting clarity of what you want to be known for that aligns to your values is the baseline. Then you can be open to what is next and evaluate how it provides an environment to align your skills to those principles. There are different seasons of life and of careers. The criteria of importance shifts depending on those seasons, and they are closely woven. The balance of work and "other" (pursuing a degree, raising a family, being a caretaker for a family member, leaning into adventure and travel, and so many more) are not always even on either side of the scale. Know what *you* want or need but also what your team and organization want or need and support them in those shifts. Be clear on how you, as their leader, want to connect to them regardless of where they land in their next role.

Julie Bloom spent ten years as a library media specialist in middle and high schools with a degree as a reading specialist, a skill set she did not apply to her role. While the role was enjoyable, it failed to really stimulate her to want to stay long enough for gold watch status—the old tradition that tenure in big organizations was rewarded with a gold watch after many years. Julie decided to go back to school. She had taken a computer punch card class in college and decided that computers were the path she wanted to pursue when she got serious about creating more options for herself. Her interest in pursuing a master's program in computer science was derailed when there was not a program for her to enroll in proximity, so she was forced to enroll in a second Bachelor of Science program to obtain the necessary knowledge and skills.

This pivot from her first career path led her to find a course she loved with a professor who saw talent in her and encouraged her to pursue the degree in computer science. She was then hired into the IT department at a prestigious university, one of the few women in the highly male dominated department and campus. She retired after thirty-five years serving in many roles, leading diverse teams and functions as the program executive officer (one of the top two positions reporting to the CIO) and leading areas like cyber security that did not even exist when she launched her career. The highly matrixed natured of the organization allowed for Julie to explore different roles and progress with so much opportunity.

Kathleen Mills knew as early as her memory serves that she wanted to be a leader, not a position like a CEO, but to affect change and bring people along. During her sophomore year of college, Kathleen received a leadership scholarship. Not really knowing what that entailed or why she had been awarded, it heightened her awareness to what her goal of being a leader someday really meant to her. She graduated college with a job in her degreed field—and hated it! She stuck it out longer than she wanted to try to make it better and shift her perspective. Courageously, she quit after a year and a half without a next step. She paused, moved back home, and instead of targeting a company, she targeted a city to see what it had to offer. After moving to the DC area, she scoured the business journal from her alma mater to inquire about possibilities for employment. One name in the directory worked at the FBI and took her cold call via old school corded phone predating mobile phones and email. He accepted her request for fifteen minutes to talk in person. She arrived eager to maximize her in-person fifteen minutes to learn as much as she could about what he did and decipher if that was interesting to her. Their conversations were mutually engaging, so much so that two hours later she left the office having established her interest, credibility, and a job offer. She accepted the offer, which became her entry in the FBI laboratory. The entry level learning of how to process evidence exposed her to agents who then testified to their findings in court. What she produced had to be sound and irrefutable. She applied the same tenacity and fervor to the job itself as she did to the process she designed in acquiring the position. She became known as *the* go-to person to get things done—especially when things lacked structure and process.

Kathleen moved through the organization, influencing outcomes and tackling more complex work. Her notoriety as the go-to person in the lab followed her through the ranks and into other divisions, earning promotions and new challenges. Learning and adapting her career progression, Kathleen was still anchored in her clarity to be a leader—not motivated by a title or position but a characteristic of leading people. Senior executive service (SES) is the top level in most government agencies covering policy, managerial, and supervisory positions. Kathleen's clarity of striving to be a leader earned her that highly sought-after rank of SES seven before she retired. That clarity served as her path.

Remember Randy with deep integrity in "Pause to Show Up"? Early in his career, his company offered a voluntary mentor program. Randy eagerly signed up to match with a mentor to shorten the learning curves and share insight with him from experience. He chose someone he found to be open and honest, super frank, and a bit aggressive. He was curious about her career because she had navigated non-linearly across several divisions, bouncing between technology and business and operations and successfully growing and progressing upward.

At his first session she jumped right in, stood at the whiteboard poised with the dry erase marker, ready to make indelible marks on the board to capture Randy's response as she inquired, "How high do you want to go? When you retire, how high have you been at that point?"

Having not thought about this quite so detailed, he replied, "Um, well, I want to be a vice president."

Not convinced his response earned the stark black ink against the bright white board, she acknowledged that title was important but inquired, "Why?"

"Based on what I know today, I want to lead a large organization over multiple functions and have a chance to make a difference; to set and lead the company strategy."

At the whiteboard, she connected that dark marker and clean whiteboard and wrote at the top of the board: VICE PRESIDENT. She stepped back and looked at Randy and asked at what level he was today. Again, she walked to the board, this time writing his response at the bottom. Like Picasso with a blank canvas, she artistically began adding more to the proverbial canvas without soliciting Randy's input. She was creating positions by level, function, time, and capabilities to demonstrate what he needed to master at each positions to get to the VICE PRESIDENT goal.

Then, the big question, "How old do you want to be when you retire?" and put that number next to VICE PRESIDENT.

She looked back at Randy, who was starting to catch up to where she was going on this adventure, and asked, "How old are you now?" and scribbled that next to his current role at the bottom of the board.

She added the time in each role necessary to accomplish the requirements of that step and was now adding his age at each of those wayposts. She capped the marker, indicating her painting was complete, sat down with Randy, and said, "You can do this in this timeframe and meet your goals by that age, but you need to get moving. You've been in your current role too long. Nobody else is going to do this for you. And others are convincing you to stay because it works for them for you to stay in this role."

The tough love was a shock to his system at the time, but that exercise resulted in a repeatable process and guide for him to follow. The guide provided both next steps, how to navigate, and an approach for him to create for those he mentored along the way. One of the distinctions his mentor made in the mapping session is not just getting to a level but operating at that level. That created a bonus of opportunity to really establish relationships and connect and develop other people while moving quickly toward a goal. Each milestone she had mapped he hit and would reflect on how he was giving back and influencing others. His first step to that success was when he paused and was deliberate in engaging and selecting a mentor. When an opportunity knocked on his door, there were no consequences to leaving it unanswered. But Randy paused and connected where he wanted to go and what he wanted to learn and recognized this as a significant point to align to who he was. He showed up authentically with clarity of what he wanted from that relationship and found someone to join him in figuring how to manage his own career and making the path work for him.

Fun fact, Randy did it. He met the goal and retired early and accomplished this feat between my interview with him and the book being published. His last day was on an October 31, Halloween. Randy hosted an All Hands Meeting and encouraged costumes. Randy had a lot to celebrate and recognize. This moment offered the culmination of the connections he made along the way while he was *doing* the job, not just getting to the next position. His authenticity and sense of humor belonged in this space. He arrived dressed as Elvis. He led the transition and passed the baton to his cross functional leadership team while they await a successor to be named. Then, true to character… Randy as Elvis left the building.

Remember the spoiler alert in "Pause to Show Up" and the district manager pointing his finger in my face telling me to do something that was counter to what the company direction was? I didn't do what he asked by calling on my doctors to write prescriptions for me to go on a fake trip to Hawaii, and I left the company. Jeff and I had four kids. We were not in a great financial situation, especially not one for me to leave my job. My clarity of right and wrong and what I was and was not willing to do did not have a price tag on it. No amount of money would justify doing something that was misaligned to my integrity. This was another step on my journey. At no point did I map "When I grow up, get married, then divorced I will…" nor did I have a "When my manager directs me to do something misaligned with my values I will…" But I was clear in my values, which made the decision clearer.

As for that job at my alma mater, I was offered the position, and it was a fantastic feeling to be offered such a great opportunity. I did the research and soul searching about making the move as a single mom and the implications this job would have on others. I turned it down with clarity of disappointment for me professionally, and clarity of my values and the compromise I would be making on what I valued most—as Ellie's mom. This also led to me not moving across the country and instead staying put and meeting my beloved Jeff. I asked if he would make me regret having a "no kids" dating rule—he told me *he* wouldn't, but his kids would. He is still right about that.

Sometimes the best thing to do is to support someone else's exploration. The destination is not the end all be all. The path and growth can offer as much and sometimes more than the target. And that target changes. Being asked, or being turned down, can also provide the learning or awareness we need to be informed about what is best for us. The next step doesn't have to be the last step, but it is always the next step. Who has been on your journey shining a light on possibility? Who are you shining a light for growth and encouragement to try different paths; or setting the direction for the milestone they are trying to reach?

PAUSE FOR PRACTICE

- ▶ Reflect on your career journey. What did you want to be when you grew up? What made that appealing to you? What did you think would make it fulfilling? Are you doing that? If yes, what did you do and who helped you to realize that dream? If no, what changed and when? When did you decide to do what you are doing now, and who helped you to get to here?
- ▶ Take inventory in whose journey you can be an active participant. Do not limit yourself to thinking you are too early in your career or that this person must be junior to you. What can you do to help them along their journey? Maybe it is brainstorming ideas to grow their business, or being a sounding board to talk through new ideas, or making introductions to potential clients, or just expanding their network.
- ▶ If fear did not hold you back, what would make you most fulfilled in your life? This requires being brutally honest with yourself and holding yourself accountable

for imagining the what ifs. If you were to live completely in-line with your values to be experienced the way you want others to experience you, what will you be and where? What will it take for you to take that leap? Professionally, if you are in the role or organization now, what is in the way of you showing up fully as who you want to be?

PAUSE FOR PRACTICE PAGE

PAUSE FOR PRACTICE PAGE

PAUSE FOR PRACTICE PAGE

Pause for Time

"Until you value yourself, you won't value your time. Until you value your time, you will not do anything with it."

—M. SCOTT PECK

AMERICAN PSYCHIATRIST AND AUTHOR

"I finally figured out what I want to be when I grow up," Ellie announced from her booster seat in the backseat of my car. I looked in the rearview mirror to see my four-year-old daughter's eyes locked on mine. Her clarity pinned me, but I wanted to chuckle at her use of the word "finally" at her ripe age of four.

"Really? What have you decided?" I replied with great inquisitiveness.

"A pharmaceutical representative" came out of her little mouth, annunciating each syllable with emphasis and clarity of what those words meant.

With so much opportunity ahead of her when anything was an option and equally attainable, my reply of, "Really? Why?" communicated my confusion of that being the dream at her tender age. Maybe I should have felt a little bit of excitement she wanted to do what her mom was doing, but my intuition was leading me, and I suspect even in that brief moment, I knew what would come next would not indicate that.

"So maybe I could see you sometimes."

There it was, the realization that where and how I was spending my time was not delivering the message of priority to my most important person. Her response knocked the wind out of me, and I have no recollection of the conversation or silence that followed. I do have a recollection of where I spent my time. I joined team calls every Friday morning during the prime point of getting my daughter ready for school and out the door. They were old school conference calls, long before video calls. My manager added my daughter to the roll call list (nod to great leadership that I was juggling a *lot*, and a minor call out offered inclusion and buy in from my young daughter). I did not have a choice in that call—I could not say, "Sorry, this is when I am trying to get breakfast in my child so she is set up for a great day." We made it part of our routine. And Saturday morning calls to the pharmacy to differentiate myself from my competitors meant my daughter was in tow—often in her sport uniform of the season before practice or games. Again, she became *part* of the routine. I thought I was including her, but her proclamation of her career aspirations told me I had demonstrated my priorities to her that my job was more important to me than she was.

Every day we have choices of where we spend our time; of what we say yes to and what we say no to. When we say *yes* to something, we invariably say *no* to something else. The reverse is also true. Unfortunately, the intentionality of the yes or no is often missing. Meetings are on calendars, you show up because it has always been there, and you have not hit pause to determine if it is your best and highest use, if you are the right person to attend, or if you could delegate it to someone else and provide an opportunity for them to grow.

If you put everything you do in a day on your calendar, and I look at your calendar, how obvious will your values be to me? I never intend to stump my clients with that question, but from the pensive looks on their faces, I often do. The back-to-back meetings have quite possibly become a habit, and you are showing up without purpose or awareness of your importance in these meetings. Maybe you received an invitation to join a meeting when you were last promoted, or you were working on a project relating to the call. The need or relevance has long since passed. Or your promotion should have opened the opportunity for someone else to join that meeting, but you are still going for lack of intentionally choosing and discerning where you spend your time and the value you offer and receive from it.

What does being busy signal? The merit badge is a symbol of achievement designated by the Boys Scouts of America. Earning these merit badges comes with varying degrees of difficulty and includes studying and completing tasks. The badge is then adorned to the uniform to wear proudly as a recognizable achievement. The back-to-back meeting culture has become the "merit badge of busy"—touted as an accomplishment as if it implies significance or status.

Over coffee with one of my mentors and valued colleague, who is also the senior executive of a nationwide leadership development firm, we were sharing the comings and goings of our lives. He relayed that he had been busy, but when I challenged to provide more of an explanation than "busy," he paused and replied, "Good one." Then he said, "Challenge accepted."

As the months have accumulated since the challenge, he has shifted two things. One is his language of "busy." The second is where he spends his time to define his days, which informs the quantification and qualification of his days. The shifting of awareness about where he is spending his time has also manifested in *how* he is spending his time and the value of both.

I asked another client, a partner at a global consulting firm, if I looked at his calendar, would I be able to tell what his values are? The pregnant pause between him articulating how his family is his greatest value and thinking of his calendar reflected how the two were not aligned. He went further to tell me how he takes his laptop on every vacation. He might not take it out of the safe, but he takes it with him. He shared this, reflecting on what message that action gives his family and how he had not thought of his willingness to compromise uninterrupted time with his family and the temptation to let work take over.

Remember DOC, our career Ford guy who modeled leadership of language that brought people along? As we learned in "Pause to Connect," he is a connector. The thing about connecting is it takes *time*. And time is not a readily available commodity, nor is it a renewable resource. Investing in getting to know people proved to be how he built teams and was able to deliver results that mattered in timeframes that seemed unreasonably quick. When the demands for where he spent hours or even minutes intensified, DOC was intentional about how he spent those units and who he spent them with. Sometimes it was just a few minutes on the front or back end of a meeting, it might be interspersed with work, or it might be setting up social gatherings to collectively watch a football game after work hours. But his purpose in any of these was using the time to learn about the people he was working with. As a secondary benefit, he created the space for others to get to know each other as well.

Time works in increments, some obviously longer than others. We measure in days of a work week, we look at weekends as the break in the hurried day-to-day, and we talk about a lunch hour. But any measure of time can have impact. Julie, whom you met in "Pause for Your Journey" at the prestigious university IT department, has navigated the highly matrixed organization to fill the lead of the software development for this part of her story. In this role, she had the task of leading the conversion of over seven million lines of code in one system and getting all of it transferred over to a new system, all before the year 2000 rolled over. The problem became obvious and a priority to tackle in 1993 because the systems were programed based on code that did not recognize years as starting in anything other than 19—, so Y2K was going to wreak havoc. Seven years may seem like a long time, certainly on this side of the new century, and we now know everything did not shut down. But on that side of the date change, this was a big challenge and a highly discussed concern as the elusive 1/1/2000 date neared.

Tasked with the code conversion and coordinating the systems, Julie had a deadline with a critical mission, but the first thing she did was to get to know each person as an individual. She did not focus on them as a group. Instead, she invested in each person one to one. Time was ticking, and Julie knew prioritizing the individual relationship building would provide insight to being more effective—slowing down to go fast. She knew who was on her team and could put them in the best role to play to their strengths for the success of the project. Through her connection tour of getting to know the individuals, she found two team members who had a long tenure in the organization. They were both older and looking closer to retirement than to learning new coding languages. Their interest in new technology was low at best. Instead of keeping them in positions to be frustrated and fail at their work, she worked with them to find meaningful roles that contributed to their individual success as well as the team success.

Time is measured in how we experience value—regardless of duration. Julie capitalized on seeing ways for individuals to be seen as contributors to overall success, which is the compound effect of spending time intentionally. In "Pause for Your Journey," we saw how Randy's mentor mapped his path to retirement with time in role and time to do the job, not just get to the next position. We have to look at the broad picture, then at the immediate moments, to be definitive in what we say yes or no to.

When we say yes to something, intentionally or unintentionally, we are saying no definitively to something else. In the case of the partner taking his laptop on vacation, he was saying yes to the possibility of working and taking away the time with his family. That message was not one he intended to deliver. He shared how he did not want to say no to his family, but by taking the laptop, he was signaling he was open to interrupting plans and letting the work seep into the prioritized family connection.

My partner in building internal coaching programs told me for years, "Do one thing well instead of two things terribly." This lesson scaled to how we both coach our clients to approach their days and times. The Russian proverb of this is, "If you chase two rabbits, you will not catch either one," and is on the opening pages of Gary Keller's book, *The ONE Thing*. In it, he lays out how to focus on that one overarching goal and the tasks to reach it in order to drive results. The premise of this approach is to focus. Do that one thing, and do it well. Don't multi-task or try to do both poorly. Doing one thing is centered in intentionality (Keller and Papasan 2012).

Hearing text messages ding while joining a video call while working on a deck for a proposal while hearing the doorbell ring is enough to distract the best of the most focused personalities. The same is true for each of these distractions while trying to have dinner with your family or watching your child's activity or playing a family game. Most of those interruptions require very little brain power and seem easy enough to pivot between, but what are you conveying? Are you aware you are conveying something even if you are not doing it intentionally? When we say yes to something, we automatically say no to something else. And this is where the intentional alignment of what you want to be known for, how you want people to experience you, and how you want them to feel from their interaction with you can be compromised or diluted.

PAUSE FOR PRACTICE

- ▶ Do a calendar audit. Look at where you are you spending your time. You can color code meetings that you lead in purple, meetings you don't lead but join in blue, family and friends in green, exercise in yellow, administrative stuff (errands, expense reports, and so on) in orange.
  - ◆ Are you clear of your purpose at every meeting you attend? If not, what will it take to validate that it is the best use of your time?
  - ◆ Are your boundaries aligned with what you want them to be? For example, are you fully present at dinner with friends or family, or are you taking calls while you are also trying to engage over dinner?
  - ◆ Now pull out your values from "Pause to Show Up." What value is aligned to each block of time on your calendar? Example: If family is one of your top values, how and where are you spending time on your calendar that maps to that value?
- ▶ Recognize the frequency of your use of the word "busy." Find another word to use in its place that others can indicates significance that others can relate. (Example: If you say you are busy, does anyone know if that is

good or bad? If you say meaningful or fulfilling or overwhelming or exhausting, you are now sharing the impact.)

▸ When you do your calendar audit, identify one thing that can be delegated or eliminated to better align to the representation of who you are as a leader. This works for juniors in organizations too: Look in the reverse of opportunities you want to have and grow into. And it works in your personal life too: What are tasks or duties you are looking after that can be shared?

  ◆ Is there a task someone else has not done before and it provides a growth opportunity for them?

  ◆ Is there a meeting someone else can shadow you and join instead?

  ◆ Is there a meeting you are going to that is no longer relevant for you to join and you can communicate why you will no longer be joining it?

PAUSE FOR PRACTICE PAGE

PAUSE FOR PRACTICE PAGE

Pause to Empower

"A leader takes people where they want to go. A great leader takes people where they don't necessarily want to go, but ought to be."

—ROSALYNN CARTER

AMERICAN WRITER AND ACTIVIST

FIRST LADY OF THE UNITED STATES 1977–1981

"Hey, Corey really wants to babysit Ellie so that we can go on a date. How is your Wednesday night?" When Jeff called in the middle of my workday to ask this, I truly couldn't believe he was both asking me on a date *and* had a reliable babysitter secured. Said reliable babysitter was his middle child, and the thirteen-year-old was known for her gift with kids—remember her from "Pause for Laughter"? This was a luxury that didn't exist in my single parenthood world. And having a teenager babysit you as a five-year-old is a rite of passage that should never be surpassed, so this was a win for me and my daughter.

Sadly, Wednesday came, and Jeff called this time to say his ex-wife had gotten wind of the plan through Corey's excitement, and she was not on board. It was early in their post-divorce life, and Jeff dating was new to everyone. And I was new to dating Jeff. She thought it was confusing for Corey to babysit the daughter of someone who he was taking on a date. It didn't matter it was Corey's idea that she presented to her dad. Jeff conceded and abandoned the plan of using her to babysit for us to go on a date. The gut punch was big.

I did keep the babysitter—one thing all the adults seemed okay with was Corey babysitting for Ellie, so long as it was not for Jeff to take Ellie's mom on a date. Why should a qualified teenager miss out on an opportunity to make some money, and what five-year-old doesn't love having a cool teenager to look up to and have some fun with and get a break from being parented? The lack of alignment among the adults about a date was not cause for punishment to the kids, and I was clear from the start that I wanted to be consistent with Corey. If I took her off the babysitter market for a night, I would honor that commitment.

There were a lot of transitions to be sorted as they scripted their post-divorce life interactions, not just Jeff's dating. As part of the transition to that new life, Jeff and his ex-wife decided to keep the traditional summer vacation with him taking their kids the first week, both parents overlapping for a couple of days, then mom staying the second week. So weeks after the babysitting debacle, Jeff was traveling with his three kids for this summer vacation trip, and he asked for a ride to the airport. Happily, I picked them up, loaded the car, and headed to the airport listening to their excited

chatter about going to their favorite place—"Summerhouse"—
with their mom's side of the family. I dropped them at the
curb with their bags, their anticipation, and a little baggie
of flight entertainment for each. The call a couple of days
later reported their mom thought the magazines, silly putty,
and snacks I sent was me overstepping my boundaries as
his girlfriend.

Fast forward six months: Corey had a middle school dance
coming up. She recently complimented me on a necklace I
was wearing—not a high value one, but crystal beads strung
together on a fishing line like wire that my sister-in-law had
made for me. We were driving home from school talking
about the dance, I offered for her to borrow the necklace if
she wanted and if she didn't have something else that worked
with her dress. Two days later, I got the call. I should have
been expecting it at this point, but I didn't see it coming. Jeff
let me know that his ex-wife had called asking him to meet
her for coffee. Over coffee she shared her disapproval of me
offering to loan a necklace to their daughter for a middle
school dance with the defense of "What if I had something
special for her?" I had, again, overstepped my "boundaries,"
which still were not clear, but I kept finding my way out of
them and receiving a message back about the disapproval
of me doing so.

The individual moments began connecting to me, and I
created a clear meaning and message that it was less about
crossing boundaries and more about there not being a role
for me. The position available was as Jeff's girlfriend—to
be a part of his life but not a part of the lives of the three
humans he was dad to and was most invested, proud, and

engaged. The roles were taken by Mom, Dad, and Mom's partner, and the neon NO VACANCY sign was flashing. Without a position, I lacked the opportunity and ability to connect with each of the kids in a meaningful way. The avenues I tried to demonstrate my willingness were met with feedback that felt harsh and sharp. These three kids were impressive, even at their young ages. I attributed that to the strength and character of their parents. Yet the conduct I was experiencing did not align with the attributes I had accredited to either of them, especially their mom. It felt like her goal was to shut me out and to punish the father of her kids and ultimately her kids by not being able to have a full relationship with their dad and who he chose as his partner. It seemed so hard to imagine, but her actions and the monologue she was communicating through others were telling a description that would be hard to hear otherwise. The lack of empowerment I experienced was defeating.

I had been faced with these same situations just a few years earlier when my ex-husband introduced his boyfriend to our family. I chose to create a space for him to add his strengths to our parenting team. The boyfriend created his own traditions with my daughter and their own relationship in addition to the one we enjoyed collectively. There were outings and firsts that I thought I would enjoy with my daughter but didn't because he or they did them. But I chose to embrace how she was having these opportunities instead of the alternative of trying to keep her from enjoying a full relationship with him and with her dad. While my ex-husband's relationship with this boyfriend did not last, the relationship my daughter and I both built with him has and continues. I didn't get it all right, but I did get that right.

These choices exist every day, all day at home, in the board room, and in the office. They are often overlooked or missed, but they are the moments that tell others who we really are.

Remember Mr. Fabey from the second-grade classroom in "Pause to Show Up"? Advancing in his career to the educational leadership roles he holds, Joe is frequently coaching others in the districts he serves. He was charged with coaching a teacher who was not meeting expectations. He clearly saw she was going to get fired. He used his coaching approach to empower this colleague to explore what would make her happiest and where she would be at her best. The ongoing conversations opened the options to this individual for her to realize leaving for something else she truly wanted was best. Empowering the individual to engage in what was possible saved the difficult exposure of being fired and instead had the desired outcome for all. Joe leveraged his connection and made the choice to empower this person and meet her with respect and input to their outcome.

In "Pause to Connect" we first met Nadia. She has spent more than twenty years developing people, processes, solutions, and relationships in support of organizations improving their talent—skills, engagement, and retention. She has a reputation of spending time with people on her team and sharing knowledge and information to upskill them. She then empowers them to make decisions and execute in their role to progress to higher levels. She is known as a highly sought-after mentor and has a following of people who seek her counsel and support. She is direct with her feedback, and she is open to the hard messages she relies on from others.

Nadia doesn't tell people, "There is no role for you," in her actions or in her words. What she does is show people what is needed, challenges her biases and perception to ensure she is not the limitation, and partners with them to strive for the best—for herself, the individual, and the company. The result is a team and a company that performs beyond expectations with connection to the vision and values.

"The way I show up is to reach out to the individual one to one, build that relationship, and ensure that they feel part of the solution when there is the possibility of differing opinions or perspectives. When there are nay-sayers or people who don't agree with the decision needing to be made, I bring them into the solution to drive it forward. I lead with empathy. I dial in how I would feel if someone was giving me the message." This has returned rave reviews for Nadia.

A few years back, there was a consultant in the business unit Nadia supported who needed to be let go from the organization. This exit hit at a time Nadia was developing one of her more junior people on her team. She invested in her team member to prepare her to lead the discussion and handle the separation. Nadia was on the call, but the teammate led the conversation, and it went as smoothly as planned and practiced, so smoothly that the consultant who was separated sent a thank you letter—to each of them. Years later, Nadia saw the consultant at an alumni event for the firm they had since both left, and more thank yous followed with the message it was the best thing Nadia could have ever done for her. She went on to share, "You and the more junior member led with such empathy and thought about me as an individual, and that was so impactful." Developing someone junior to her empowered that individual to handle the hard discussions along with empowering them to think about their career differently to ensure they found the right fit for their skills—the compound empowerment.

Product design director Gloria R. was still pursuing her media management degree several years ago when she traveled from her native Germany to the Netherlands with little English and no Dutch skills. She went to fill an internship with a television show as a creator and gain exposure to production. Upon her arrival she learned the television show did not yet exist, so she would instead be an executive assistant assigned to a print magazine—nothing of what she agreed or set out to do for the three-month duration. Also a surprise was the lack of Dutch language competency expectation in the job posting. A few weeks into the post, her lead's growing annoyance that Gloria still did not speak the local language was palpable An interesting approach this manager took was to then only speak to Gloria in Dutch, which could be either a hierarchical power play or a submersion language exercise.

Gloria was then tasked with a written assignment about London to be completed in English. She completed the article and received feedback that it was terrible. She did not have a great grasp of the English language at that time, so that was one hurdle in itself. But when she inquired for further feedback, she received none. The manager she was assigned to offered no input and no mentoring. As a young student early in her professional life, Gloria was shy and unsure how to navigate the many dynamics in a role that did not match what she had applied and traveled for.

Three months passed without much beyond making morning tea for her manager every day and being given no direction nor opportunities. This approach to empower a student who was willing and ready to learn about an industry fizzled when the supervisor stopped engaging with her after the first disappointing assignment and omitted direction. Media internships were in great demand for the flood of students seeking to fill them, with the need far outnumbering the available positions. For students to take them on a "volunteer" basis for the sheer experience to secure the spot was not uncommon. This one was unique, though, with a contracted 200€. Month over month resulted in no paycheck and a growing concern for timid Gloria. At the conclusion of the internship, Gloria earned nothing, not one cent, with the defense that she did nothing. She showed up for a position, had it switched on her, gave it a shot, accepted some thin and negative feedback, and was allowed to wither on the vine.

Gloria did find the gumption to face her employer and make her case for the impact this would have on her scholarship and stand by the contract they had agreed. Ultimately, Gloria received the money she was owed per the contract with a strong message from her boss about how grateful she should be for the manager's "generosity."

When we pause to think about the experience we want someone else to have, we often shift our approach. These are the times that catch us by surprise when someone says, "You have touched my life in a way that has a positive impact on me," in reference to moments we may not remember. Being connected enough to your values and knowing how you want other people to feel can and will drive how you show up.

When other people feel our impact, they are empowered to do something and more to drive their own impact.

After more than twenty years and a lot of life events later, the early days of my dating life with Jeff are easy to Monday morning quarterback. Calling the plays that should have been called for a game that has already been played does not demonstrate skill, talent, or character. From my perspective, I felt a lack of empowerment to find a path with my stepkids, whose lives I was eager to define a role in. The angst caused by my not being able to find an "in" led to a lot of failed attempts and excessive learning in conflict styles, which are hard memories. Except for one conversation, all of Jeff's ex-wife's communication filtered through him. Had she communicated directly with me—set the vision she had for them and engaged in a conversation with me about where my strengths were to bolster her, my gaps where I could learn from her, and how we would venture this journey together from a place of love—it would have had a much more productive and inclusive impact for us all.

Often, we do not realize when we are inhibiting the opportunity to empower others as we navigate what we see as the next step on a path. The pause for opportunity to empower, delegate, engage, and allow another to occupy a space is quite possibly inhibiting someone else from a feeling of belonging—and limiting your own as well.

Where are you prohibiting someone else from growing or belonging? How does that fit with your narrative of needing your own belonging?

PAUSE FOR PRACTICE

▶ Capture your reflections of how it feels to be empowered and the impact. Notice who are you developing and partnering with, professionally and personally.

- How do your rate your feeling of belonging on a scale of one to ten?
- Do they feel empowered?
- Are you providing enough direction?
- Who is empowering you?
- What more do you need, and what is in the way of you asking for that?
- What are you willing to do to increase your rating of one to ten?

▶ Building your brand and reinforcing it requires consistency. Whether you are being shadowed or you are building a new team, when something needs to be done quickly and it is in your skillset:

- Are you pausing to think about who you can teach or have shadow you before jumping in to do it?
- Where can you identify opportunities to allow someone else to do something you could do to allow them a growth opportunity?
- This is not limited to work. Who might you make room for in your family or personal life or friend group?

▶ Who is empowering you, and how are you taking the reins to engage and grow?

PAUSE FOR PRACTICE PAGE

Conclusion

"Believe me, my journey has not been a simple journey of progress. There have been many ups and downs, and it is the choices that I made at each of those times that have helped shape what I have achieved."

—SATYA NADELLA

CEO MICROSOFT 2014–PRESENT

"You know, Momma, at first I wasn't so sure about that Dr. Broker. But I sure have grown to love and trust him." Ellie gazed out the window of the car door Jeff had just shut after buckling her into her car seat. As I put the car into gear to drive away from our house, and he was getting into his car to go back to his, her announcement six months into our relationship startled me. How a five-year-old could articulate that type of clarity about her relationship and the attachment she felt was mind boggling to me. How she felt such a strong connection was not. Jeff has the capabilities she needed to fill the open position as her stepdad. She gave him consistent feedback that he was more of a father to her than her dad was and even offered to promote him by inviting him to adopt her. You've made it this far, so you deserve to know the good part: Jeff adopted Ellie when she was fifteen.

The blended family journey is in fact a journey, and ours continues. I continue to learn and grow in my opportunities to embrace Frankl's moment between stimulus and reaction in "Pause to Show Up" to own my choice in how I want to be experienced and how I want to experience the moments and the journey. I can't change the moments I missed—and there were many along the way—but I can own each one going forward.

The moments along the way resemble the scattered breadcrumbs. As leaders navigate, you have the opportunity to be intentional, which is to symbolically pick up the breadcrumbs on the path pointing to your core values, signal to your brand, and what people can consistently expect from you. When you are not clear or aware of your choices, you might be picking up someone else's breadcrumbs and conveying a much different persona than you intend.

Imagine being at an offsite meeting with your senior leadership team. The shared ride app keeps canceling after you are matched with a driver because the distance you need to go is not very far, so it's not as valuable to the drivers as a longer distance. A peer hears your frustration and shares they put in a further destination, and then when they get in the car they change the location. This approach solves for the problem of getting to your destination, but what is it conveying about who you are, and how clearly is it conveying that message? The leader who shared this with me about their peer felt a strong disconnect in values and saw this person as dishonest. It's possible this peer sees themselves as resourceful and clever and values that.

It is hard to imagine anyone promoted into a senior role sets their intention to create massive destruction and harm so that their successors spend years "cleaning up the carnage." Yet these behaviors and legacies are in every industry and somehow survive. What gets in the way of realizing you are that person? We asked, "How can this happen, and why is it still happening?" It doesn't have to, at least not with the level of frequency it currently does. And that is what encourages good talent to leave organizations—lack of leaders they see themselves modeling and leaders who do not demonstrate boundaries for intentional brand aligned connection. You don't have to be a casualty, and you now have a resource to aid someone else to ensure they are picking up *their* breadcrumbs and are following their path.

Moments slip past us too frequently without us noticing we made a decision to respond in a way that signals to others who we are. This may be holding fast to your boarding spot in line for a flight and not letting someone in the same boarding group ahead of you; or your reaction to someone trying to merge into your lane on the highway; or the language you choose when speaking about yourself; or your reaction to an email of a colleague announcing their departure from your organization; or your level of conversation you engage while walking through a corridor of colleagues junior or senior to you; or a request from a neighbor for some help while you are in the middle of something else. Independently, these seem benign and insignificant moments and are among millions of others like them. Yet each one is an instant that adds to the other observable responses to paint the visual of you. Recognizing moments to *pause* and consider what you do next, and how that weaves into the fabric of other actions observably about you, is the distinction to make. These behaviors are what create the environment for ourselves and others to thrive.

What gets measured is what gets rewarded. If organizations say alignment to core values is how promotions and bonuses are determined, but the performance appraisal process looks at metrics that are more concrete like lead conversion or utilization, there is a mismatch. People will not only be confused, but they will work to what is measured not what is espoused. This is your call to action for what you espouse, what you hold yourself aligned and accountable to, and what you demonstrate for others to measure. This applies to being the up and coming leader as well as the seasoned one; it applies to the stepmom and to the mom; and it applies to both sides of all the coins of who we are and the roles we fill.

The nine pivotal options in the moments to consider the impact how you connect to others, what you choose to align to your values, and how you honor your needs, beliefs, and values. The control of what or how others experience you is not guaranteed, but when done intentionally there is a high probability your inward connection to your choices will articulate a clear outward indicator of the same.

When you *empower* others, you are connecting to share knowledge, time, capabilities to offer an opportunity for them to grow and ultimately mirror your contributions.

Spend your *time* being intentional and keenly aware for what you are saying yes to—and in return what you may inadvertently be saying no to because of that yes.

Focusing on the *journey* indicates you are present, staying in real time, assessing what the current opportunities are, and taking inventory of what is and is not working for you right now and what options you have to chart your next move.

Forgo the priority of others to focus on your own sense and security of *belonging*. If you can't see yourself in those you are surrounded by, then you can't fully show up and be your best self. Leadership is not something that can be faked, so belonging and feeling a connection or creating one enables the servant side of your leadership to flow.

Embrace *laughter* in a lighthearted and inclusive way. The subtle nuances that can go unacknowledged or can be called out to create a shared moment of humor creates connection. And a good laugh can change a day for the better.

Make the choice to *connect*—are you a bait or a bobber—to get meaningful rapport *for* and *with* you. There is no need to be lonely or isolated.

There is a need for *clarity* in prioritizing the goal or the relationship. Determine which is more important to you, and ensure your approach to conflict resonates with you and with others as a demonstration of that importance.

There are easy and excusable options in word choice and omission. The *language* you choose represents you and delivers a message. Aligning it with your authentic self can be a barrier or an invitation for others to connect, follow, or resist you.

Ultimately, *show up*. Be the person your intuition and character calls you to be. Feed that ob-servant leader in you to serve yourself and then others and know your brand. Then make the choices to honor your brand.

The action subtly (possibly too subtle) woven through this book is the need to reflect. And when stress is high, demands are competing, you feel isolated or like the chips are stacked against you, or little to nothing is in your control—those are the times to dig deep into the reflection. That is when to take inventory of the moments and how you show up and if you did it with intention or let the moment pass without a pause. None of us are going to get it right all the time—and that is okay! Neglecting the practice is not.

This book serves as a guide to call you to pause and embrace the moment to be clear in your thoughts, actions, and impact. The practices are intended to honor who you are and who you want others to know. This will generate a new level of awareness that will begin to seep into your psyche. This is not a check the box, read, do, close, and put on a shelf book. Open it. Reflect on your practices. Engage in conversations with others (another way to connect and find your belonging). What changes when you go back and reflect on the "Pause for Practice" sections a second time and with a little more insight and awareness? What feelings arise for you to name and notice? What evidence do you have to measure the alignment, or disparity between, where you want to be and who you think you are? How can you validate that? Self-reflection is positive and requires discipline. The courage is in opening up yourself to be vulnerable enough to hear the hard feedback from yourself and others. Equally hard and necessary is to hear the positive feedback. How you talk to yourself matters!

The biggest challenge of writing this book has been putting on paper the stories that involve many others and respecting the impact to them while honoring my experience. It has been an active practice of aligning my values and brand with how this will be received and navigating my sense of belonging in this family and my current and future clients. My work, day in and day out, with leaders navigating their own vulnerabilities and trusting me in the partnership encouraged me to push on, as there is great value to creating our own belonging. Belonging is something we don't often measure or plan for. Instead we just hope or assume we will feel the reciprocity of connection.

Our blended family includes four accomplished adult children in healthy, loving, trusting relationships and a zest for life, adventure, and laughter. This is my hope for them, and I admire their boundaries. I had one "rule" when I was a single mom before I met Jeff—I would not date anyone with their own kids. Remember that in "Pause for Your Journey"? When it was clear we were falling fast for each other, I asked him if he was going to make me rethink that rule. He responded, "No, I won't, but my kids will." And they did. I still hold regret for even creating that "rule." What rules have you put in your path as unnecessary barriers to success, belonging, and connection?

Annually refresh your practice. When you are navigating change, transition, low points, high points—anything that is a clear diversion from the norm—it is a good time to refresh and capture what you are noticing. Which of the areas of focus are most challenging to you—time, connecting, clarity? If you are resisting one, it is probably a good place to spend extra time and reflect. Pause to reflect and capture what is and is not working and how you will incorporate that as you navigate the moments ahead of you.

Finally, what are your stories where you experience these pause opportunities? Where have you learned from blending families or leading organizations? Who are you sharing those stories with?

ACKNOWLEDGEMENTS

Would you rather train for a marathon or write a book? That was my soul-searching question for the first half of this journey when I was training for the Marine Corps Marathon and jumping all in to write this book. While I did both at the same time, I realized how similar the commitments and experiences are to each other. Both take a lot of perseverance and endurance, and neither can be done well without a team of support. The marathon itself is filled with supporters and cheerers along the route. For a book, you, the readers are that support system. So to you - thank you. Thank you for picking up this book and for reading what I have put on paper.

To my biggest and by far most fun hype man and relentless supporter of everything I do, my one and only Jeff. I wouldn't have this lens of expertise if not for you - thank you for offering me the position and investing so much in my development to succeed. I pick you. Forever and then a little longer.

To my Ellie - being your mom is what I am most proud of in this world. I aspire to be more like you every day. Your support, encouragement, and involvement in this book has been yet another Mommy and Ellie adventure. Thank you for providing humor and content to always keep me on my toes. And to my Es, thank you for being fully engaged and engrossed in this process. Your fingerprints are all over this and I love that.

To my parents for instilling an early resolve that I can -and should- do anything and affording me some of the most amazing experiences and opportunities to learn and grow to be who I am. Thank you, Mom and Dad.

To my brother - you have always been the loudest voice cheering me from the sidelines. I will never stop doing things trying to earn your cheers. T- thank you for being the constant encouragement.

To Robyn, Corey, and Scott - while I have yet to get clarity on my role with each and all of you, my support, admiration, and love for you has never waned. I am proud to have you in my life and that you are the package I got when I married your dad.

To my BAMRs who were both marathon and book supporters in ways I didn't know I needed, but you did and somehow always do, thank you.

To the many people who gave me their time and trusted me with their stories to form this book. The time spent with each of you continues to inspire me that we have good people in this world who are living into their purpose. And to those who read the early and rough versions, provided input and walked the delicate balance of feedback to help me get it "right". It was a big ask and I learned so much from each of you. Nellie, Joanne, Pravin, Joe, and Sharon - your dedication to read and re-read, get into the messiness with me, and to provide 11th hour suggestions and edits was beyond compare. That experience took vulnerability to a new level, thank you for keeping me "safe" in the process.

And to Jon, who over a cup of pour over coffee told me I had to do it—you have some mad influence skills! I am so glad you were on the author journey with me. We did it!

To the Manuscripts Team who made this possible and put my insights into publication. Special thanks to Beth Anne Macdonald, Cassandra Caswell-Stirling, and Chrissy Wolfe who made sure I didn't lose my voice or my vision.

To my presale supporters who believed what I would put together in this book was worthy of your interest. Your early confidence provided me the encouragement to continue…. and accountability to finish!

Greg Billings

Jonathan Tuteur

Sarah and Claude Billings

Marie Carr

Rebekah Vint

Stephanie Ross

Cindy and Reid Goodwyn

Susan Gentile

Patricia Sasser

Julie Campbell

Teever Handal

Marshall Makaila

Dan Fisher

Maureen Moore De Mott

Jess Kruckeberg

Lindsey Burgess

John Fitzgerald

Elton Ndoma-Ogar

Laura Young

Ellie Broker

Pam Gaither
Stacey Rutherford
Leela Magosin
Pete Tunnucliffe
Jeff Broker
Matt and Catherine Miller
Nellie Viner
Mary Alice Nichols
Meg Ferguson
Michelle Ozanne
Arianne Rice
Jennifer Martineau
Nadia Krivickova
Sharon Justice
Debbie Hellman
Kristine Cordova
Emily Cheeseman
Cady North
Kimberly Garley-Erb
Pravin Raj
Margaret Enloe
Ashlee Magosin
Sartaz Ahmed
Tibbie Farnsworth
John Riedy
Billy Christensen
Megan Carpenter
Adam Cox
Paula Levy
Lynn Howie
Jesse Jacoby
Jill Hill

Denise Poth
Sonia Louise Lapinsky
Kristin Stevens
Shawn Mick
Amanda Nolan
Sheila Heaphy
Paul Damiano
Robyn Mayer
Rachel Verlik
Paige Ryan
Harrison Fanaroff
Jody van der Goes
Olivia Mathijsen
Jen Sanders
Shereen Sater
Jon DAlessandro
Darrin McCall
Vanessa Tennyson
Celina Mohovich
DeDe Esque
Jeff Moody
Janel Loud-Mahany
Brennan Jones
Jenny Kruckeberg
Eric Koester
Sierra Stevens
Bobbi and Jeff Noe
Deanna Steele
Susanna Kondracki
Conor McShane
Margaret Bush
L. David Ashby

Kathleen Mills

Glen Miles

Travis Ellinger

Calvin Cribbs

Shelley Jensen

Caroline Adams

Michael Thaxton

Megan Pace

Joanne Spigner

Elisa Dorsh

Kristie Kauerz

Lyne Desormeaux

Maren Perry

Joe Fabey

Lynn Bowman

Beth Crumpton

David Begin

ChyAnn Conley

Judy Fellhauer

Sarah MacGuire

Adam Meiras

Sydney Richeda

Andrea Sunset Weslar

Emily Kokenge

Amy Martin

Terri Smith

Keith Warren

Susan Suslow

Russ Kumar

Richard Quincy

Scott Pankoff

Leslie Deacon

David Radford-Wilson

Jenny Williams

Meredith Trunkett

Donna Kennedy

Ann Pearson

MaryLynn Roush

Ellen Ericson

Doug Zawisza

Brenda Wilkins

Felix Pflaum

Becky Bunn

Rebecca Weaver

Shelly Thieme

Rosa Williams-Lu

Carrie Holtz

Charlotte Haims

Jonathan Roth

Beth Weissman

Amy Bjork

Maggie Echols

Kelly Ross

Heather Backstrom

Jules Benson

Ellen Trager

Jenniffer Pak-Collins

Katherine Richardson

Sharon Houghton

Emmy Timberlake

Appendix

INTRODUCTION

Siddiqui, Mohd Moid Abdul, and Ayesha Farooq. 2019. "Mergers
and Acquisitions: Failures and Causes, an Evidence-Based
Approach." *International Journal of Interdisciplinary
Research and Innovations* 7, no. 2 (April–June): 147–152.
https://doi.org/10.1108/S1876-066X20140000030004.

Tessema, Mussie, Goitom Tesfom, Marcy A. Faircloth,
Mussie Tesfagiorgis, and Paulos Teckle. 2022. "The 'Great
Resignation': Causes, Consequences, and Creative HR
Management Strategies." *Journal of Human Resource
and Sustainability Studies* 10, no. 1 (March): 161–178. DOI:
10.4236/jhrss.2022.101011.

United States Census Bureau. 2023. "National Stepfamily Day."
September 16, 2023. https://www.census.gov/newsroom/
stories/stepfamily-day.html.

PAUSE TO SHOW UP

Andert, Darlene, George Alexakis, and Robert C. Preziosi. 2019. "The Millennial Effect: A Multi-Generational Leadership Model." *International Leadership Journal* 11, no. 2 (Summer): 32.

Baker, Coleman A. 2018. "Between Stimulus and Response, There Is a Space. In That Space Lies Our Freedom and Our Power to Choose Our Response. In Our Response Lies Our Growth and Our Happiness." *Colemanbaker.org* (blog). January 24, 2018. https://medium.com/@colemanabaker/ between-stimulus-and-response-there-is-a-space- ad5261e3c74e.

Greenleaf, Robert K. 1970. *The Servant as Leader.* South Orange, New Jersey: Robert K. Greenleaf Publishing Center.

Jones, Sandra. 2019. "Leadership Lessons from Satya Nadella." *Chicago Booth Magazine* (blog), The University of Chicago Booth School of Business. January 10, 2019. https://www. chicagobooth.edu/magazine/leadership-lessons-satya-nadella.

PAUSE FOR LANGUAGE

Burkus, David. 2015. "If You Want to Be the Boss, Say 'We' Not 'I.'" *Business Communication* (blog), *Harvard Business Review.* March 6, 2015. https://hbr.org/2015/03/if-you-want- to-be-the-boss-say-we-not-i.

Hougaard, Rasmus and Jaqueline Carter. 2018. *The Mind of the Leader: How to Lead Yourself, Your People, and Your Organization for Extraordinary Results.* Boston, MA: Harvard Business Review Press.

Johnson, India R., Evava S. Pietri, David M. Buck, and
    Roua Daas. 2021. "What's in a Pronoun: Exploring
    Gender Pronouns as an Organizational Identity-Safety
    Cue among Sexual and Gender Minorities." *Journal
    of Experimental Social Psychology* 97 (November): 1–14.
    https://www.sciencedirect.com/science/article/abs/pii/
    S0022103121000974?via%3Dihub.

Pennebaker, James W. 2011. *The Secret Life of Pronouns:
    What Our Words Say about Us.* New York, New York:
    Bloomsbury Press.

PAUSE FOR CLARITY

Thomas, K. W. and R. H. Kilmann. 1974. *Thomas-Kilmann
    Conflict Mode Instrument.* Washington, DC: APA PsycTests.
    https://doi.org/10.1037/t02326-000.

PAUSE TO CONNECT

Brown, Brené. 2022. *The Gifts of Imperfection.* Center City,
    Minnesota: Hazelden Publishing.

PAUSE FOR LAUGHTER

Barker, Lynne A. 2017. "The Science of Laughter—and Why
    It Also Has a Dark Side." *Science and Tech* (blog), *The
    Conversation.* April 17, 2017. https://theconversation.com/
    the-science-of-laughter-and-why-it-also-has-a-dark-
    side-76463.

Kong, Dejun Tony, Cecily D. Cooper, and John J. Sosik. 2019.
    "The State of Research on Leader Humor." *Organizational
    Psychology Review* 9, no. 1 (February). https://doi.
    org/10.1177/2041386619846948.

Rosenberg, Caroline, Arlene Walker, Michael Leiter, and
Joe Graffam. 2021. "Humor in Workplace Leadership: A
Systematic Search Scoping Review." *Frontiers in Psychology*
12 (July): 3–40. https://doi.org/10.3389/fpsyg.2021.610795.

PAUSE FOR BELONGING

Doyle, Glennon. 2023. "Kelly Clarkson: Red Flags, Divorce &
Starting Over." *We Can Do Hard Things*. Released June 12,
2023. 55 minutes. https://wecandohardthingspodcast.com/.

Greenleaf, Robert K. 1970. *The Servant as Leader*. South Orange,
New Jersey: Robert K. Greenleaf Publishing Center.

Maslow, Abraham H. 1943. "A Theory of Human Motivation."
Psychological Review 50, no. 4 (July): 430–437. https://doi.
org/10.1037/h0054346.

PAUSE FOR YOUR JOURNEY

Luce, Carolyn Buck. 2022. *Epic! The Women's Power Play Book*.
Austin, Texas: Lioncrest Publishing.

PAUSE FOR TIME

Keller, Gary W. and Jay Papasan. 2012. *The ONE Thing: The
Surprisingly Simple Truth behind Extraordinary Results*.
Austin, Texas: Bard Press.

Author Bio

Megan Broker is an executive coach whose mission is to empower leaders to enhance their self-awareness and influence, enabling them to drive greater effectiveness and positive change. With a career spanning nearly three decades marked by award-winning corporate roles within the telecommunications, pharmaceutical, and consulting sectors, Megan has solidified her reputation as a beacon of guidance and transformation.

Megan's superpower is quickly establishing rapport and resonating deeply with those she encounters. Throughout her career, she has exemplified her dedication to guiding others toward a meaningful alignment with their values and igniting their inner compasses to lead purposeful lives.

Megan lives with her husband in Colorado. She is a proud mother and stepmother, whose journey continues to unfold amidst the enchanting complexities of blended families. Through these experiences she embraces both the joys and challenges, perpetually discovering the magic in the messiness of life's intricate tapestry.

www.ingramcontent.com/pod-product-compliance
Lightning Source LLC
Chambersburg PA
CBHW070900160726
48004CB00003B/1174